e.s.p.

THE AWFULLY BIG ADVENTURE

I

If you cannot teach me to fly, teach me to sing.

J. M. Barrie, *Peter Pan*

THE AWFULLY MODEST INTRODUCTION

I don't want to spoil your enjoyment by giving too much away about the following essay, which I wrote ten years ago, feeling very glad to be of use. Reading this piece again, after not bothering for all of those ten years – the last line of the piece was a sort of promise I ended up keeping – I see that I was as worried as I would be a few years later when David Bowie died that my role in life had changed. I was being forced to move on from being a music writer specialising in original, if for some highly irritating and random, thoughts. I was being asked in a professional capacity for my opinion about rock stars, mostly those that had died, but my particular answers weren't the ones wanted or expected.

The kind of rock critic I had been on and off since the late 1970s was once powerful enough to be in control for better or worse of the music's creative and cultural direction, taking responsibility with a few others for the shape and content of its past, present and future, for working out the great moments and anointing the greatest acts. At the beginning of the twenty-first century, this form of excitable, diligent critic had yet to be fully replaced by Amazon recommendations, streaming algorithms, concentrated Wikisummaries, blunt talent-show judges and voters, oceans of shared playlists, music forums and online reviews with their scattered, customer-friendly stars. But the change was already happening.

The more I was asked by the mainstream media to comment on the death of a musician, especially in the aftermath of the sudden death of Michael Jackson in 2009, the more I could see the change coming. Oddly, music wasn't as intensely culturally significant as it once was now that it was becoming important for everyone and more or less freely available. As certain hierarchical structures and systems collapsed, traditional gatekeepers were being replaced by ghostlier, actually more tyrannical if well-intentioned gatekeepers. Even though I was being asked questions as an apparently qualified expert by the media when a music star died, it was at a time when the once-unassailable authority of the self-certified expert, with their grand claims, obscure knowledge and arcane explanations, was rapidly diminishing. The voice of the crowd, the weight of plain, hasty opinion and levelling enthusiasm, was taking over, and as someone allegedly with the correct experience being booked to appear on programmes and impart hard-earned knowledge, I was actually expected to be more of a professional mourner, an entertainment therapist, discreetly wailing undemanding, sentimental grief and on the side adding a few calming factual details that could easily be scraped from the featureless, uninspiring if very helpful Wikipedia.

I was there to help the wounded collective gather for a shared moment of heartbreak, where the talk needed to be blandly but appreciatively of 'tragic loss' and 'will be terribly missed'. Adding any personally applied critical dimension or complicating, contemplative conceptual texture to the response was not particularly welcome, because after all in the eyes of the interviewer I was just making it up, dealing in unstable theory, and was likely to be greeted with quite angry suspicion, even disgust.

The rock critics, with their moody, all-knowing attitude, their often wilfully esoteric interests and snobby derision of the herd mentality, had been dragged via technological democratisation into the increasing hostility and resistance towards the so-called intelligentsia, the controlling, self-perpetuating elite – even though the better rock critics tended to feel they were for the underdog, the marginalised, radical outsider, dedicated to championing those who crashed through borders and progressively rearranged the artistic environment. Critics were being chased out of town, especially now that a too easily activated social media released millions of voluble new voices into the world, to clean things up and point out alarming, contaminating inequalities, injustices and scams, or make an unholy mess of reality because it couldn't be worse than what had come before.

I wasn't really interested in 'the news', only, perhaps, the news that stayed news. I wasn't really interested in the basic facts, certainly not now there were all the facts being repetitively collected online and automatically laid out as if they were a greater help to the world, what the future would be made of, reduced to siphoned, targeted content.

I wasn't really interested in whether someone liked something or not, as that was neither here nor there – it didn't tell me much about what they liked or didn't like, and why it had been made and how. I was interested in what was elsewhere, in working with ideas, beyond the repeated, settled facts and the simple truth that people liked some things and didn't like others. For me, this 'elsewhere' was the enigmatic, elemental space where the music came from, it was where those making the music were working; elsewhere, in the dark, outside of the facts, which became fixed and restrictive, outside of the fan's neediness, which became a matter of market research, of commercial formula and public relations.

After he was found dead and morbidly displayed on the sort of rampaging news and web channels revelling in such occasions and scanning for pundits to deliver some safely neutral if moderately emotional sound bites, I was more interested in wondering: who or what had killed Michael Jackson? This was no normal death, and no normal person, no normal superstar. This was absolutely elsewhere. I wanted to answer the question at length, not in the few minutes, or even seconds, I would get when asked by a busy, distracted on-air reporter about the 'importance' of Jackson, intolerantly stamping down on any flights of fancy or high-and-mighty, self-regarding rock-critic myth making. I wanted to take it seriously in ways the news coverage was not interested in, as they started to cover popular culture after years of being mostly indifferent outside of the general clichéd sex, drug and suicide shame. I wanted to deal with things cosmically, not cosmetically. That had been my job, once, and in my head still was.

A periodical published in 2009 by Faber and Faber titled *Loops* gave me a chance to answer the question, at length, and begin to understand what I actually thought about the life and death of Michael Jackson, pop's bizarre deity. *Loops* didn't last long. It was a temporary, last-ditch attempt to rescue the imperial idea of the rock magazine with its egotistical writers, intense, speculative reviews and rampant printed pages, because the rock critic was now nothing special, and in the age of internet-conceived democracy, anyone could have a go and have their say. For an issue or two, it was just like the neither good nor bad old days, where things weren't better, they were just very different. A time when a relatively small selection of superior-feeling rock writers roamed the late-twentieth-century rock planet acting like they owned it, using words, and lots of them, to create a constant forward-looking sense of excitement and discovery, until they ran out of steam, or ran out of places offline to dictate their taste, supervise history, manufacture scenes, promote cults and create the canon with little competition.

Again, without giving too much away, it is clear from my thinking in the following piece I wrote for *Loops* who I felt was responsible for the sinister death of Michael Jackson, and probably clear in this introduction, with all the clues that have appeared since, that I haven't really changed my mind.

The answer to 'who killed him' lay in some science fiction place between Jackson himself being the culprit, and the rest of us also being to blame. You might not count yourself as part of 'the rest of us', but the truth is we all were, all of us who consume and are consumed by popular culture, eventually everyone, watching his life sloppily, nastily end, after what seemed a few years of cliffhanging close calls, from whatever vantage point we adopted. Whether obsessed fan, with enough activist, almost artistic commitment to his cause to be a combination of follower, stalker and lover, possibly driven totally wild by the fanatical nature of your identification, or more of a passive, part-time fan, liking in a low-level, uninvolved way the heat and sweetness of a few of his songs, approving of the way he passed on instructions with an exile's grandeur and outcast dignity about how there was absolutely nothing wrong with being, or feeling, really weird and turning the whole world into a permanent children's retreat because you simply don't know how to cope.

Maybe you had fond memories of when he had, through song and dance, record and TV, through mingling possibilities, found his power and faithfully escaped a dark past, turning eccentricity and struggle into commanding, life-enhancing exoticism as others had from Louis Armstrong through Thelonious Monk to Nina Simone.

The time when he was musically on top of the world, plunging upward, using fantasy to fight against banality, a fleet-footed, brilliant-minded, smart-mouthed model of prejudice-battling optimism, dressed to the glittering nines, free within himself, his switched-on gestures plain from the back row of arenas, spurred on to wonderful feats of the imagination, gracefully helping his fans coalesce back into the condition they needed to be in to deal with their own damaged, disjointed lives.

Beneath the surface, so he sang, relying on a certain amount of trust, of ornamented innocence, we are one – as though the moral urgency and raised consciousness of the 1960s civil rights freedom struggle could be funnelled through the creative, spiritual and commercial development of his eclectic, adaptive performance and positively influence all aspects of American media, entertainment and culture. The hope he brought, the idea that blacks and whites would listen to the same music, where everyone whatever their background should be free to dream, would surely never keel over into hopelessness.

He was so soft, smooth and cool with a provocative body defying indifference to rule and order. A white angel with black wings floating high above mundane earthly concerns, in the thrilling days when his life seemed to have some form, his music, for all its accessible gloss, defined American grain and his performance articulated and transcended the grim surrealism of modern American blackness. Those final, elevated years, as he approached his late twenties, before he seemed to be always under attack, bullied for being too black or not black enough, for being celibate or over-sexed, for betraying his heritage of rhythm and warmth, charged for the grotesque state of his poor defeated, auto-dissected body, for his pathetic tantrums, his phoney, watered-down songs and thunderous ignorance, his fading powers, decadent vices, wasted excellence and defective morality.

His only response, we were told, was to install himself in a neglected mansion, make up horror-show renderings of comforting domestic bliss, crawl into bed with groomed, dazed versions of himself, gorge on candy bars, snort pixie dust, drown in cartoons, play with dolls, talk to the animals, curl up in a frightened ball, crave an anaesthetic, cry himself to sleep, stain his pyjamas and mostly miss out on daytime. All that early charming breakthrough black promise turned into nihilistic, conforming mimicry of narcissistic white excess. Delightful little Motown maestro singing his heart out nimbly dancing on the edge of time out became rotten, devious fiasco deep in conversation with himself, hands and voice trembling like water. What the hell happened?

Maybe you were relatively indifferent but sort of distantly curious as to what on earth his warped once-in-a-lifetime life was actually like – what did it feel like to be Michael Jackson; what did he see in the mirror, swimming out of his eyes? Or you were a member of the scavenging, argumentative media who helped encourage his opulent self-destruction and hounded him to an early death by recording, and distorting, the details of his career and personality and alleged strange perversity, determined to reveal his deepest, darkest secrets because, so they said, their readers and viewers deserved to know. It was, as they liked to say, in the public interest. He meekly gave them everything cruel, mainstream journalism is interested in, especially, of course, at the end; the unusual, the sensational, the improbable, the melodramatic. To some extent, the media was what the hell happened to Michael Jackson, with all of us implicated as consumers and subscribers.

The media began invading Jackson's privacy from when he was a showbiz teenager, as if he was dabbling in alchemy, acquainted with malevolent forces, as though they saw something alien and diseased crawling across him. He was brazenly trespassing into an area where he didn't belong, and therefore they decided he had to be closely monitored. He generated a form of unspecified but actively popular energy that seemed to be mocking them. What was he hiding up his sleeves? The media took him hostage, as they do to such characters when they've got nothing better to do, which is most of the time, thinking maybe of course that black sins, and the sins of those that stray from their straight, colourless, fearfully protected set-up centre, are worse than white ones. He was guilty, until proven dead.

We were all caught red-handed with a weapon in our hand, and a sort of motive, even if we just wanted to put him out of his misery, and take away the pain, of being publicly loved by so many but never actually loved, it seemed, in private, which you could always feel whenever you heard one of his songs or saw a photograph or video, his blazing nerves magnificently turned to patterns on a screen. You heard a voice full of life and naked desire, and somehow also dread, and saw a dead-eyed man-child with a startling glassed-in face who could move like few others, as though it could be a way to feel safe in his own skin, which was always conspiring to wrong-foot him.

We were all working as a team to destroy this shadowy, transitional being. Watching him, doing nothing, while he beat himself to death dancing.

Perhaps some of us, including the victim, just couldn't

stand it anymore – the chaos increasingly marking the life of a mere entertainer, even this extraordinary, transformative entertainer who turned out to be better off dead, where he didn't have to try to maintain the absurd illusion of stardom under continually ludicrous and farcical circumstances. There were famed entertainers before him who had recommended one way or another through the performance, the event, the after-party of their death that the best way to sustain a certain sort of stardom and avoid having to hellishly repeat forever their own early heights of inspiration was to die. To start singing with the voice of the martyred dead, transient forever. Or, as the phrase started to become in the ten years after Jackson died, take control of their own narrative – in the only way that made a real difference, so that their legends can grow.

The messiness and meanness of life has a way of ruining the bright, fantastic light of fame; life gets in the way. For Jackson, a seemingly successful life was increasingly filled with problems, addictions and frustrations. All that trivia, all that negotiation, all that ageing, and decaying, all the compromise, the lingering trauma, all that living up to impossible standards, moving yet again from the comforting dark into a harsh, unforgiving spotlight, being surrounded by invented versions of yourself, thousands of visions and revisions, that end up being more real than the real you which is unreal. It's not good when your dream is to make life a fantasy and act like you're a king, and then you realise that your dreams are not coming true, but the nightmares are, and in fact the idea you are a king is nothing but an act. You might as well act like a Disney princess, just as close as being a king to who you are, or who you want to be.

You can spend, lavishly, because you're made of money, where once you were just looking to get paid, as though the achievement of individual wealth fulfils Martin Luther King's dream of equality. Your house has a hundred rooms, but you can't buy happiness. You can't find your way home, and you spend most of your time in hiding. You're stared at like you're sinking into dementia, but that's no excuse for all the logic-deprived ghastly errors you've made. You're endlessly auditioning, always needing to find a new adventure, a new way of moving, sounding and finding yourself, of glamorously not being normal, and others have learnt from you, and start to do better in the auditions.

They have sharper routines, flashier sequins, dandier rhythms, pushier representatives, edgier collaborators, cleaner drugs, spookier opinions, fewer injuries, all that fucking auto-tune and those mega-numbered YouTube followers, a slicker, hipper take on rewiring normality and boosting their persona, and seem more what audiences want, what they need.

You're being relentlessly tested and insulted. If you're only as funky as your last cut, you've lost the game and you don't know why. You don't understand the din and hum that surrounds you. You've forgotten where you came from; the crackle and dust in the grooves. You've lost sight of the race you're in. You're in the distressing dark, feeling the world being devoured by Snapchat speed, and a deluge of rhymes and beats, baroque hightops and opportunist slogans, reality TV meta-stars, millennial amnesia, endless hyped-up sequels and internationally marketable franchises, sentimentally dazzling juke box musicals and make-believe controversies, all of which seem somehow to have something to do with what happened to you.

You can't imagine what's about to happen in the decade after you die, even as you'd recognise it all, because you predicted it, seeded it, mixing entrepreneurial image-making élan and imaginative determination. It's all just repeats really since the final episode of your show. Coming after you, as the progenitor of modern entertainment action: parallel styles, energetic reflections, nostalgic reboots, a few rip-roaring forgeries, similar pretence and definitely similar forms of posing and pleasing, however original, globally exaggerated by the insta-technology of the times and the liberated pressure of the newly untethered, directionless masses daily plotting their escape, hypnotised by pixels, authoring their own performance and recording their journey, their never-ending party.

You were ahead of your time in the way you rejected reality, and replaced it with whatever came to your mind, enacting all sorts of ritual to get what you wanted, treating media as a kind of art form: you can be seen in the loony bragging and sulking of cockeyed Kanye believing he was Yeezy; the lotioned swing of Frank Ocean, the luxury edge of Kendrick Lamar, the family-friendly, good-time risk-taking of Bruno Mars, the calculating star power of Drake, the constantly transmitted post-Wacko decline and fall of Chris Brown of *F.A.M.E.* and *Fortune*; the slow dissolve of Johnny Depp; the narcotic off-beat teen sensation of *Fortnite*, the realigned joy and history of the flamboyantly civic *Hamilton*; the world-wrecking trash-and-grab reality twists of illiterate evil libertine Donald Trump with his TV eyes, the flash-and-grab tele-hallucinations of avant-garde storytelling superhero Donald Glover; the flirtatious, elevating frenzy zones of Beyoncé; the empty, philanthropic billionaire promises and betrayals of Mark Zuckerberg, his wealth apparently the price of progress; the world-wide screen power of the pale, pale Dragon Queen, the earth-bounding pomp and ceremony of *Black Panther*, all the corporately sanctioned, diverse freak-saviours and electrifying villains in the expanding Marvel Universe, and the oddly timed deaths in your mysterious spirit of Prince, Whitney Houston, Amy Winehouse and George Michael. Death keeps going through the motions. Death wins hands down. All that commerce, and distraction, all that fun and fame, carries on regardless. Some jump forwards and others fall back.

After all, in this dubious digital age, in a world out of control, inside an ever-flowing social media stream, where refugees are going nowhere, children are ripped from their families by Americans following orders, suicide bombers are wrecking neighbourhoods, prisoners are tortured, nations are hacked, privacy vanishes, is wilfully renounced, the imagination shrinks, literature is debased, bullies and emojis rule, shit happens . . . without the celebrities, their attracting of attention, the famous, the amazingly vain, the notorious and noxious, the skin-deep YouTube gurus, the red carpet regulars and the award nominees, without their comings and goings and various doings, without their stories and the gossip that surrounds them, without their rhymes and costume changes, their talents and flaws, their changes of mind and body, their medicated considerations, their treatment of the truth, their celebration of the self, the power that goes to their heads, what would we have to fill, and kill, time, and how would we model our own lives and grade our own aspirations?

If you'd stuck around, in all your corrupted, influential, mask-wearing majesty, pulling out from that final coma, pushing open the lid of the coffin and heading into a longer life, you'd have fitted right in, even if you just fitted in as someone who didn't fit in, as a scoundrel, a scandal, history, social climbing and fantasy turned to shit, because you exploited your fame and all the spinning space and extravagance that came with it to mess with the heads and bodies of vulnerable others. Did you think it was your right? You had no time to think.

Or maybe in the next ten years you could have proved yourself time and time again as constantly re-constructed superhuman; had headline-inducing comebacks after comebacks, appeared at Glastonbury as an undisputed legend and pop seer, made an autobiographical album with serious-artist intent produced by Kamasi Washington called *The Killing of Love*, been godfather to North West, 'owned' your own streaming site like Jay-Z, been worshipped as Pharaoh of the rising-up gender fluid, as Mahatma of Time's Up diversity, as self-help Napoleon of the mentally ill. You'd have sung some frosted gospel at the wedding of a new mixed-race American Duchess, who would have been the daughter-in-law of your close cousin in audience-manipulating cunning, Princess Diana, leading to an honorary knighthood. You'd have formed a virtual supergroup called Fairy Tale with Taylor Swift, Grimes'n'Musk, *Guardians of the Galaxy*'s Groot, Pikachu and a clone of Mahalia Jackson. You'd get your own producing deal with Netflix. You'd have swapped minds with Cardi B for some virtual Disney splendour. You'd be completely at home in a post-truth twenty-first century teeming with surgically modified human brands, psychographic marketing techniques and those trying too damned hard for the sake of their value and their own relevance to say the right thing and support the right cause. You would become more fashionable than ever as the world caught up with the madness of your advertised reality, where the idea that a lie is not a lie if the teller believes it became more and more the way of the world.

A longer life was never meant to be, even one where you could have lived a little more to see the finished portrait by the activist history painter Kehinde Wiley that you had your people commission months before your death, because you could see what was coming and were arranging your legacy. Finessing your appearance. The painting where you are presented as a king, the star of the show, surely to your exact taste, more than hinting how you saw yourself. You wanted him to paint you because you saw or were shown an exuberantly unsubtle Wiley painting at the Brooklyn Museum of a young black man posing as Napoleon crossing the Alps. That you fancied being turned into loud paint by Wiley shows how seriously you took yourself, and at the same time, how playful you could be; a combination that leads to something garish and hyper-romanticised but paralleling how majestically and heroically the madly powerful and therefore often madly corrupt traditionally liked to represent themselves. Self-serving themselves into jumped-up legend.

It's like when you met President George H. W. Bush, very proudly and yet quite matter of factly wearing a make-believe ceremonial soldier's uniform and a couple of medals that, as writer Dave Eggers noted, you probably presented to yourself. In your mind, you'd been in the wars, issuing orders and planning attacks. You'd seen action. You'd saved lives and lost a few. It was your duty to announce this by meeting the American President in the uniform of a pop star sincerely playing the role of world leader from an abstract new nation where the capital city is Google. What on earth would you have wanted to wear if you'd met the American President who turned out to be image-besotted entertainment fascist Donald Trump, the implausible pair of you convening to sort out the invention of immortality (for a select few, mostly those who wear medals or ties) in an insidiously grand gold temple designed by the flat-white artist Jeff Koons? Perhaps you would have worn a lion's head, and he would have licked you clean, removing any sticky lingering signs of troubling blackness, of gender confusion.

In the deliberately overstated Wiley presentation, which is a performance in itself, you are wearing armour under phosphorous clouds, sitting bravely ready for battle on a warhorse that seems part robot, part mythical beast as two flying naked cherubs lay a wreath of laurels on your head. Of course! The ten-feet-tall, reality-breaking painting rises up out of a history you saw yourself as becoming part of, where celebrities, royalty and presidents occupy the same rococo commemorative territory. It rocks up out of the way the baroque Flemish master Rubens celebrated Philip II in the olden days of the seventeenth century.

That picture was called *Philip II on Horseback*; your painting is titled *Equestrian Portrait of Philip II*. You are a king playing a king. You are at the centre of some story. Of the same story. It's written – it's painted – all over your captured expression where you are awed by yourself. Perhaps you are preparing for death's cold hand, for the flight of your soul. Preparing to meet a holy God as though you are on equal terms. You are no doubt about to burst into a song that makes the spirit strong, music that mourns those who are about to shed blood, or privacy, in a civil war where the battleground is Twitter and Facebook.

Wiley, committed as much as you to making up history rather than merely relaying and repeating it, known now for his portraits of President Obama, rappers, athletes and street kids, keen to champion and indeed honour what he calls 'the brown faces' that went totally missing in Western art, admitted to adding 'a little cocoa' to the skin colour you had reached at the time he painted you, at the end of things, when your complexion was the fairest of them all.

Heaven knows what fancy dress you would have worn at the awkwardly moving 2018 funeral of your father Joe, long labelled as the depraved abuser who had nine more years of simmering infamy after your demise. Maybe one of the medals you would have worn on your funeral uniform would have been for surviving, to some extent, Joe's diabolical mental and physical pressure. His death at eighty-nine led to a refreshed round of shocked stories about how he terrorised you and your brothers to the point of beating with belts (and even chemically castrating you to preserve your golden falsetto) so that the adolescent Jackson 5 achieved levels of polished entertainment precision that some always suspected required extreme parental intimidation to achieve and maintain.

A forlorn Father Joe desperately argued in 2010 – to priestess Oprah, of course, who had originally received your illuminating 1993 confessions about the menacing nature of a radical showbiz dad's disciplinarian tactics – that he was just trying to keep his kids out of jail, and on the right track. And anyway, he claimed, he never beat them, not like the media made out, he just chastised them, with a kind of idiosyncratic interior family strictness that his estranged wife, Kathleen, suggested was usual at the time, especially for an energised, male-heavy, working-class black family hemmed in by changeless racism, religious orthodoxy and social deprivation.

Maybe that strictness, and a relentless rehearsal regime that erased a so-called normal childhood, did involve a strap, for threatening show, or even a sudden out-of-scale bruising slap. Maybe treating them as his possession he did push the family pop group too much. He wanted his Jackson 5 to constantly work hard, because success would save them from poverty, from a mundane future. The apparent misery of their childhood, constantly chained to their emerging abilities, saved them from an obscure, miserable and powerless life where they were fighting just to get by – with bouncing baby Michael being so obviously the best and therefore getting the worst, and somehow in Joe's fevered mind the most loving, attention. This was his way of teaching them what was right and what was wrong, his way of fighting the seal of Satan, of building bright fantastic lifeboats that could deal with life's stormy tide. It wasn't malice, or at least, there was much more to it than mere maliciousness.

He marched them in single file, limited their options as individuals, and somehow, even though this surely contradicted the excitement that needed to be pressed into their performance, the necessary beautiful joy of their music, the essential empowering message they transmitted that growing up is fun, perhaps he instilled into them that the idea of having rules is an important part of becoming an adult. Or perhaps they rebelled against his rules, and found in performance the freedom they could keep to themselves and then parade for others.

He thought it was because of his dictatorial organisation that you were so good, but in fact it was because inside, where the real action was, you were resisting his rules. Inside, you were breaking formation, and planning an escape, desperately wishing to see the variety of the world. As you rehearsed, pirouetting in unison, building up a sweat and feeling real fear, as you followed orders and received punishment, you dreamt of another place, a place of your design, where in winter it always snows popcorn, and if the world could be like your dream, what an exciting place it would be.

All this measuring, scheming and forward planning meant you were never conventionally a child. All this messing up of being a child and becoming a teenager, this stunting of natural growth, puberty-blocking and macabre control of young energy as part of an exacting professional plan led to a piercing need lasting the rest of your life to be surrounded by children. 'I find the thing I never had through them,' you told blessed Oprah, as though this explained everything. You fed off their innocence and purity, a reminder of what was violently snatched away from you, children allowed to be children, searching for places that are safe, all of which led to other problems and a tangle of issues and children not allowed to be children, or safe, at all.

How far would the sins of the parent have carried? How would your relationship with your own three children have developed if you had been there as they moved into their teens? Would Prince Michael the First and the Second and Paris call you Dad, or Your Majesty, or, you never know, Jacko? What kind of fun would you all be having together? Were you planning a remake of *The Sound of Music*? What did they know of the stories of how Granddad Joe generated the Jackson 5?

In the few days after the death of your father and his grandfather, your now twenty-one-year-old son Prince

Michael posted a message on Instagram that may have been the sort of statement you might have made on such an occasion, or not close at all to what you or your social media managers would have said. You once said you loved your father, but never really knew him. He remained a stranger, and perhaps he would have even if you lived, however much he pleaded for forgiveness, however many times you met, to talk terms, or look for answers.

Prince Michael seemed to have got closer to Joe and found the man. In his statement he was angry at the accusations of assault, of coldness, and protective of the Jackson name, clearly getting his information straight from his grandfather – Prince was standing up for you, perhaps, but more immediately, Joe. Without the parenting style of Joe, he said, the Jackson 5 would have joined gangs, or died young and violently. He praised him as a man of great willpower. 'You taught me to take pride in the Jackson name and what it really means, you taught me dedication in the face of adversity and most of all you showed me strength and fearlessness. There is and never will be someone like you.'

If you'd lived, perhaps Prince Michael would still have lashed out at those who doubted the methods of Joe, whether you wanted him to or not. But your children were destined – designed – to be left on their own, to work out without your help the eccentricity or not of where they had come from and who and what they were. They were almost made to order more than conceived. The older they got, the harder it would be to hide from them that they were Jacksons, of those Jacksons, and what that stood for. The Jacksons that it seemed the whole world were always judging, and hating, in a world of hate. They had to get their information from somewhere, and as you were missing, Joe, the original creator, stepped in. The information might not have been as non-binary as yours would have been, but it came from the heart of the Jacksons.

You never had to work out what kind of father you needed to be, whether you needed to put yourself between your children and your father, how you might swallow the pain and let him be simply their kindly grandfather. Would you have become head of the family, Joe snuffed out for the force of his early ambition, with your wounded version of what love is taking over, for better or worse? Would you have expected your children to grow into show business, or run as fast as they could in the other direction, heading towards the radiant bliss of privacy? They didn't have much choice in the end. They inherited the family cause, and more than most children of celebrities the curse and chaos of fame, which would have enveloped them as they became more conscious of the world their father created, and their unsteady place in it.

You were not going to be around to solve any of this. It would all take on a life of its own, coiling around your

absence and presence, where your once mighty, now failing father outlived you, and took part as much as your
children in a Michael Jackson afterlife. You were heading elsewhere.

You could never have survived in a world that went
woke, that moved to call time on creeps, crooks and
tricksters, or at least the ones that were easy to catch,
because of an invasive, uncontrollable social media that
could via new sorts of leaking acid eradicate the shadows and convenient hiding places more successfully than
the old media. You'd had your time and used up all your
highs. You'd shown the way, how a life could be one episode of a constant reality show, how much all everyone
wants is to be loved, and then headed for the way out.
You were doomed in the way only someone as famous
and famously fucked up as you could be. Your world
was coming to an end. You felt abandoned and under
constant investigation where once you were eagerly
praised and embraced. Everything you so carefully built
had turned into the wreckage your life became. Your
feeble, weeping body was getting in the way. Another
screw kept coming loose.

Enough is enough. You're fed up of saying: oh no, not
again. Not me again. Not me. Oh God no. The world
is basically baffling. Death gives you a chance to start
again, to press the reset button, execute a breathtaking
edit, from here to there to blessed nowhere. You can

get rid of that body, which caused you so much trouble. You can change the shape of your family, a family that couldn't save you and that you couldn't save. A new game can begin, a spectral game of hide and seek.

Michael Jackson is no longer lonely – I say hours after he'd died, on live peak-time television, to a shining, over-confident presenter looking at me funny because he just wanted to know what my favourite Jackson song was – just ghostly. Just another strange story from the past, one that can be told in so many different ways.

II

Once you're grown up, you can never come back.

J. M. Barrie, *Peter Pan*

THE AWFULLY BIG ADVENTURE

ONE

Michael Jackson died in June 2009 from high levels of drugs in his body, including the powerful anaesthetic propofol, more commonly used on hospital patients before surgery.

TWO

I first thought, when I heard the news, how did anyone ever get to be so lonely? And yet, at the same time, the centre of so much attention, as he moved among us, sometimes so fluently, so far inside and outside his own body, using his feet to communicate with us about the miracle of light, and time, it seemed like he'd flown in from another universe, and landed in such a way that his feet were yet to hit the ground. He visited earth, and never quite connected. This lack of connection was endlessly fascinating, whether represented persuasively through the moves and demands of a sensational entertainer born to amaze, with a voice that soared God-how-high, as clean as if cut with a diamond, or through how his trapped, unstable mortal energy was ruthlessly processed and packaged as pure pleasuring product, or made grotesquely explicit through the alarming ways that his skin turned to paper, his flesh started to leak and his eyelids turned to dust.

Sometimes he moved so nervously, so awkwardly, so damned tentatively, it seemed like he was not human, or at least had once been human, and then became something else, or he was slowly, painfully becoming human, transforming from something alien and removed. Sometimes, as he moved among us, on the way from one sort of peculiar ceremony to another, with a frantically rigid look on his face, it could make you feel sad and confused, he seemed so brave and tragic, it appeared he didn't actually know what to do with his feet, or his hands, or the thoughts, agitated shreds of sensation, that must have been ganging up on him inside his head. His eyes were black holes swallowing, rather than reflecting, light.

By the end of his life he looked like this exotic being from another universe who had once risen among us, possessing a dancing body that could change shape in sudden mid-flight, and then a famous scarred body that changed shape for vain, sick reasons, a pitiful, trapped creature that had finally landed, and met the earth, not with an elegant, cushioned softness, but with a horrible, catastrophic wallop. He crash-landed on to earth, and his body, mind, sanity, vision and memory splintered, and he moved among us like an extravagantly deformed casualty that was both banal and mystifying. We couldn't bear to look at him, this 'it' containing so much devastated promise and so much visible oddness and sadness, and we couldn't take our eyes off him.

Then I thought, I suppose, now I came to think about it, that I had always heard loneliness in his voice. He was always on his own, and even at the height of his fame, the time when he seemed most alive, and in control of his self and his surroundings, he seemed distant and preoccupied. He moved among us, super present in his songs, extra vivid in his videos, desperate to ensure that the second after we'd heard him, or saw him, we would not forget him. If we forgot him, it would be like he had never existed. If we forgot him, what was the point of living? Who would ever know he'd been alive?

He desperately needed to be desperately needed, and he choreographed an existence dedicated to ensuring he would never be forgotten. He laboured so hard to establish an indelible identity, even if this meant stretching his skin and mind and sanity to such an extent eventually everything would snap. He was so keen on making sure that everyone knew who he was – so that he would feel wanted, and he sang confessional, often furious songs that exposed so much about his paranoia, insecurity, prejudices, distress and anxieties, he revealed so much about his miserable childhood, his sexual bewilderments, his emotional burdens, his eccentric desires, his diseased self-control, his macabre obsessions, his poignant dreams of happiness, his restless sentimental craving for some kind of calming religious certainty, his humiliations, his raging boasts, his terrible destiny – but he never let anyone get to know him.

THREE

The prosecution paints a disturbing picture, in which moms jockey for status at Neverland by offering up their little boys. Meanwhile, Michael is fickle with his attentions, moving on to a new special friend every year or so. There was Wade, Brett Barnes, the '93 kid. As a local writer suggests to me, 'Michael's like the Matthew McConaughey character in Dazed and Confused – *he gets older, they stay the same age.'*

FOUR

To be honest, my very first thoughts upon seeing and hearing that Michael Jackson had for certain died, in circumstances that were undeniably and inevitably suspicious to the point of seeming scripted, were professional. I thought about myself.

I thought, what the hell am I going to say, when someone asks, as they surely will, very soon, what my opinion is about Michael Jackson? I didn't think about the sad, broken man who had died in agony inside an anonymous rented Los Angeles mansion apparently located in the centre of a local celebrity-spotting route. Died in monstrously shabby circumstances facing excruciating pressure both from those that loved him and those that hated him.

I didn't instantly consider the real person dealing with the collapse of an empire and the disintegration of a reputation, the ever-accelerating deterioration of his youthful zeal, the wrecked, fastidious individual who must have still existed inside the mauled and massacred body it had become so easy to mock and marvel at. The body that had turned him into a pitiful modern freak show – more manufactured mechanical puzzle than living, breathing, feeling person – that surely made it increasingly difficult to take seriously or at least fully comprehend his once-upon-a-time actions as motivated showman, guileful, passionate musician, cryptic creative catalyst, surreal businessman and slick, knowing audience manipulator.

I didn't immediately think what the news of his death might have been covering up – the fact that he had been dead for days and now was the time, organised by business, family, television, shady conglomerate, whoever was now in control of the estate, the idea, of Jackson, to reveal the truth. Or the fact he had been dead for years and it had been decided, days before Jackson was due to play a stupid amount of live shows, that it would be more commercially shrewd to exploit a dead body, and a sparkling new show business legend, than risk the possibility that it might be spotted that

Jackson had been replaced by a slightly too eager look-a-like or a not quite paper-thin enough hologram. And then, of course, he might not be really dead at all, and this was some ludicrous trick of the light, some monstrous publicity that would lead to the news a few days later, on the eve of the fifty shows he had been signed up to play in London, that he was still alive. It was, in some way, yet another mask, another cover-up, another way of fooling us into believing what Michael Jackson, whether a person, an insurance scam, a company, a conspiracy, a small island off the coast of Mexico, a slice or two of corruption, a stubborn drain on our emotions, an array of pixels in flux, a mere pop singer with ideas above his entertainment station, wanted us to believe. I thought all this eventually, as you can see, but not in those first moments after I had seen and heard the news.

FIVE

What is Michael Jackson according to Google #1

Michael Jackson was whipped into shape by his father
Michael Jackson is a freak
Michael Jackson is soooooo sexy
Michael Jackson is #1
Michael Jackson is back
Michael Jackson is a weird motherfucker
Michael Jackson is a father again

Michael Jackson is black?????????

Michael Jackson is in 3D

Michael's father performed with The Falcons

Michael Jackson is a dance

Michael Jackson is Joan Crawford's daughter

Michael Jackson is leaving Sony

Michael Jackson is the worlds leading consumer

Michael Jackson is a way of life

Michael's mother is a God fearing Jehovah's witness

Michael Jackson is still a werewolf

Michael Jackson is dedicated to bringing Michael Jackson fans worldwide all the latest and official news surrounding the king of entertainment

Michael Jackson is saying when you're strong and you're good, you're bad

Michael Jackson is beautiful

Michael Jackson turned down a part in *Men In Black*

Michael Jackson's birthday is August 29th

Michael Jackson is the whole business of money and sex mixed up with something primitive and deep

Michael Jackson is confessing to Oprah Winfrey

Michael Jackson is a eunuch

Michael Jackson is jealous of Eminem for being able to play the MTV game the way he'd always wanted to and in tears when he sees Eminem make fun of him

Michael Jackson is innocent why did he pay off the witnesses he makes fantastic music but he should not be above the law

Michael Jackson is pictured at the University of Oxford Union

Michael Jackson is the king of hearts and the king of music

Michael Jackson is alright

Michael Jackson's Smooth Criminal is the seventh single from Michael Jackson's *Bad* album

Michael Jackson is one of a kind

Michael Jackson is only at home on stage

Michael Jackson is a southerner

Michael Jackson is actually a cyborg sent from the 24th century to halt the current trend in music

Michael Jackson owns the bones of the Elephant Man

Michael Jackson is mentally unstable? yes/no

Michael Jackson is more than just an extraordinarily popular singer and wonderfully gifted dancer

Michael Jackson is a hoax

Michael Jackson does not clean his own house

Michael is taking his milk of magnesia

Michael Jackson is saying that he respects the obligation of confidentiality imposed on all of the parties to the 1993 proceedings

Michael Jackson vividly speaks their thoughts and dreams

Michael Jackson needed plastic surgery to restore his appearance after suffering horrible burns filming a Pepsi commercial

Michael Jackson is debatable

Michael Jackson is realising how the debris of the past
   and present can be salvaged to make up a different
   identity

Michael Jackson is clinging gingerly to the bobbing
   raft

Michael Jackson has reached the lying in state stage
   where it remains to be seen if his remains will be
   seen

Michael Jackson is saying 'I was a veteran before I was
   a teenager'

Michael Jackson is poured like ketchup over everything

Michael Jackson was fourteen minutes long with a
   beginning, middle and end

Michael Jackson and all that shit is ass backwards

Michael Jackson was born in 1958 in Gary, Indiana

Michael Jackson is bewildered at the lengths people will
   go to portray him so negatively

Michael Jackson is being teased and ridiculed by his
   father

SIX

First of all I couldn't help but wonder – as a journal-
ist and broadcaster, knowing that I would soon receive
calls from various parts of the media asking me to comment on radio shows, and TV programmes, and in print
– what my position was in terms of his music, his image
and reputation, his existence and now the non-existence.
The non-existence that would now mean an endless,

horribly sincere parade of those randomly appointed broadcasting judges and insiders with a point of view on just how heroic, or perverse, or exceptional, or irrational, or *compos mentis*, or just plain medicated he really was. Did I have a point of view? I wasn't sure. I just knew that I was about to be asked, and really, whoever would be doing the asking didn't really want any kind of answer other than one that just filled some time and added to the atmosphere an amount of whatever was required to ensure that the atmosphere surrounding this news struck viewers as being given the circumstances more or less correct.

SEVEN

The defence calls Lisbeth Barnes, the mother of Brett Barnes. She says she let little Brett go on tour with MJ all over the world. She let Brett sleep in Michael's bed the entire time. She's asked why she let Michael sleep with her son. 'Why not? You just feel when you trust someone and when you don't, and I had total trust in him.'

She says she discussed with her husband whether it was appropriate for Brett to sleep with Michael – but their only concern was whether Brett would be imposing on Michael's privacy.

EIGHT

Within minutes of the announcement that Michael Jackson was dead the news flamed across the insatiable web, the increasingly undead news channels, the intimately connected social network, in a blast of gossip, supposition, sympathy and composed shock, the result of perhaps his most ostentatious move as commercial artist since the 1982 NBC TV *Motown Special* moonwalk. (The moment when he most perfectly expressed in astounding motion his celebration of America – and the American dream filtered through black history, minds and bodies.)

It was also apparent that the future of Michael Jackson as item, icon, aura, memory and pure self-referring information was going to be fought over by a toxic combination of those acquisitive hustlers swiftly racing across the headlines and tweeting and mourning and lamenting to claim with best stricken expression put first that they knew him best. The history, reality and commercial future of Michael Jackson were being claimed by those who found themselves in the best and nearest position to take possession.

Obviously, this meant his family, or at least the still-functioning, visibly show business part of it that relied on Michael to give the Jackson name any enduring credentials, because even though to some extent Michael was a has-been, past his best, deeply creepy, all but totally done in by an excess of attention and indifference, the family itself without him was useful for very little apart from appearances on reality TV shows. This once mighty show business family without Michael and everything he brought with him was a little lifeless, verging on the completely empty. Not even Janet, the Jackson sister that had seemed to maintain a certain physical and emotional balance despite being a Jackson, and at times a radiant singing and dancing star with something magnificent on her mind, could help maintain the Jackson brand to the extent the family were used to.

It was Michael who helped sustain whatever interest there still was in the Jacksons as a financially viable show business family, however far he exiled himself from the family, however distant he was from that particular faded circus. Michael drew attention to the family, as the member of the Jackson 5 that most confirmed that glorious early promise and maintained possible future interest in any kind of adult version of the group, and as the most visible and obvious sign of what can happen to an immature, innocent young kid inducted, willingly and yet against his will, into show business.

He was the one male member of the original Jackson 5 singers, Michael, Jackie, Tito, Jermaine and Marlon, who ever had a sophisticated appreciation of the pop business. Younger brother Randy arrived later, once the Jacksons had left Motown, signing in 1975 with CBS's Philadelphia International Records. He replaced Jermaine, who was married to Motown chief Berry Gordy's daughter. Randy had more of the multitalented Michael aptitude for wanting to write and play, although Jackie would also write, and occasionally even sing a lead vocal. Michael, though, was the dominant lead voice, and the lead imagination. He was the freak amongst them, possessing the sort of anomalous energy that can mutate into genius. Michael had an instinctive get-up-and-go understanding that to succeed and then succeed even more in a business that was all about the latest craze and distributed craziness, and then to keep on succeeding, even if everyone else thinks you are failing, involved much more than just a mere musical talent.

It involved an economic, psychological, cultural, technological and political reading of just how the myths of fashion and music work, and an ability to invent yourself, and reinvent yourself, in ways that kept pace with changes in expectations and trends. Whatever else Jackson was, he was definitely an analyst, once spectacularly accurate, and gradually a little off the beat, and then finally fairly out of focus, of his own position in the public imagination and how to adjust it so that he always featured prominently in that imagination.

Michael was the most inquisitive and purposeful, he had the sharpest aspirational visions, perhaps because he had been weaned on his father's almost vicious need to improve his family's lowly status and rank, and he had been educated inside the streamlined Motown school, where self-styled black capitalist Berry Gordy Jr had pulled off the modern miracle of selling joyous, free-thinking black pop music that didn't completely betray its roots in defiant gospel and mercurial rhythm and blues. Michael, so the story goes, forced the divorce from the controlling, cautious Gordy, and encouraged the Jacksons' move to another ingenious soul-based commercial corporation, run by the studio designers of the deeply beguiling tough and tender Philly soul sound, Kenny Gamble and Leon Huff. (Gordy and Motown kept the plain but undeniably alluring name Jackson 5. The boys were now, even plainer, and never as fabulously, the Jacksons.)

Michael became fascinated watching Gamble and Huff write and record, closely witnessing how they dealt with musicians and operated the mixing desk. They happily shared with him their experiences and techniques in the recording studio, the way you could experiment inside it as though it were a laboratory, work on different ways to stack and manipulate vocals, and their uplifting soft-hearted themes and messages for songs, the love, unity, harmony, togetherness, would have a strong influence on Michael's more plangent, heartwarming songs.

Working, hard, with Gamble and Huff was a significant part of the education of Michael Jackson, making him appreciate the part the recording studio would play in realising those ambitions he had, inspired by the more adventurous Motown acts, to succeed not just as a performer and interpreter but as a writer and studio technician. This opening up of possibilities and an acquired technical expertise prepared him for his partnership with his greatest showbiz sidekick, Quincy Jones. Meanwhile, the rest of the Jacksons never followed their brother into the pulsating wired-up depths of the recording studio, where true magic could be found, and reproduced, and rewound. That was for others. That Michael wanted to be one of those 'others' who could play with sound, and learn how mental energy could make it on to tape, and use sonic possibilities to enhance and finesse a song, to supply it with an amount of distinctiveness that could emphasise its commercial appeal, was one of the things that separated him from his slacker, weaker and much less interesting brothers.

Disciplined in the arts of self-improvement against unruly American odds, never doing enough to please his disciplinarian father – driving and bullying Michael with as much exploitative hard-boiled money-making zeal as Leopold Mozart did with his own weirdly bright young son Wolfgang – and then never doing enough to please himself, to live up to his own standards of excellence, Michael developed the most ruthless iconoclastic ambitions. He had, even if initially reluctantly, done the kind of homework that the rest of the Jackson boys had evaded. As one of a family group, he was inspired from the very beginning to find ways to stand out, to not just be A Jackson but to be The Jackson, to sustain the factors, even if just that he was the youngest and cutest, the fastest and snazziest, that made people single him out. He could not lose, once he grew up, whatever amazed audiences because he had such stunning natural skill as the kid. Once he grew up: he had to find ways to rec-reate that initial sense of shock and delight people felt when they saw him as this supersonic ultra-cute boy.

He studied what it takes not only to transform your compulsions and manias into sound, but also how to match that sorted sound with a combination of dance and appearance and a physical hint of mystery that helped brand you, and make you noticeable. The rest of the Jacksons took for granted that there were those who could do this for you, but Michael approached the formatting and framing of his own personality and charisma with forensic attention to detail. Working out what kind of character you were selling yourself as was as much a part of music as the song and the dance, and inventing this character so that it appealed to the right kind of audience requiring a certain sort of pleasing was both an art and a science. Michael got it. He was very good at it. He was so good at it that it would run away from him – he became addicted to the giddying, gratify-ing process of changing his image, trapped by his own appetite for constantly proving he was ahead of the rest, always the antic pop pioneer. Constantly establishing his difference, because being different, for better or worse, and therefore free, was everything that he was about.

He worked out that success in the music business involved constructing plausible facades, and that imper-sonating, or replicating a form of sincerity was actually more useful and durable than simply being sincere. You shouldn't be too nice, but you should seem to be very nice. You should charm the public without it seeming that you were using nefarious means to charm them, and thrill them without it seeming that you had desperately rehearsed to the point of blankness the exact gestures you would utilise in order to thrill them. There was a fakeness about the whole thing, a fakeness he had a special relationship with, because he had been a kid faking being an adult, and he seemed to understand how to achieve and maintain this fakeness and disguise it with fluid levels of sincerity and controlled, diverting spontaneity.

He had the ability to motivate colleagues and fans to believe in his talents, ultimately a slippery, agitating skill as a kind of illusionist convincing those around him, and eventually that number ran into the millions, that he was exactly what he pretended to be – the king of pop. Without Jackson's professional and metaphysical agility as he mutated from enchanting teen idol to challenged adult superstar, it was unlikely that the other Jackson boys could have lifted themselves out of the '70s as anything other than a shrivelled nostalgia act acting out their alert, fancy hits with frayed cabaret glibness. As Michael fulfilled his plans, his schemes and dreams, and succeeded in moving out of the disco-daft '70s and into the different, tricky, image-mad '80s as though he himself was in control of the whole new decade, he dragged the rest of the Jacksons with him, even if he didn't particularly want to. He extended their lifespan a few times over, even as he fell from the sky.

As Michael plotted his wild rise, and suffered his wilder fall, as the plot twisted way beyond his control – or was it all part of his plan, if we decide the plan was sort of cosmically conspiratorial and way beyond the realms of reason, the graphic wished-for outcome of all this convoluted manipulation of his and his fans' desires? – the Jacksons were always a possible gateway to Michael, and therefore still had a use for a media chasing sensational, squalid or stupid news about Michael and his strange ways. As soon as Michael died, the Jackson show business family received a jolt of much-needed energy, and quickly adapted to their new position as grieving keepers of the sacred flame and proud protectors of the imperial image as if in the end this had been their purpose all along – to be the dignified collective widow, the conscientious organisers of the tributes, memorials, souvenirs, films, the controllers of the posthumous career. He'd fought so hard to fight his way out of the family's claustrophobic, blackmailing control and assert his more bohemian independence that in many ways it had killed him. Now safely dead he returned to the bosom of the Jackson clan, as much a member as he had been in the days when he was the darling showy tiny one in the Jackson 5.

NINE

The defence calls Karlee Barns, who is Brett's older sister. She's the smiliest, bounciest witness yet – a cute young lady with darling dimples and a twinkle in her eye. When asked to describe Neverland (she, too, has been staying at the ranch while she's here in town), she sighs as she says, 'Every time I go back it feels like I'm going home.' This elicits a group 'awwww' from the fans at the back of the courtroom.

TEN

Then there were those that were in place very quickly representing themselves as close friends of Michael, the special few that knew the 'real Michael', who had the virtual diamond-encrusted key to his heart which they naturally kept close to their heart. The key to revealing that you knew the real Michael involved confidently confiding that the soft, fluttering voice Michael used in promotional public, as part of a much greater distraction, a more serious sleight of hand, was nothing like the way he usually talked. The voice he used when he was playing himself – so there was such a thing! these self-styled close friends said so! – when he was issuing instructions, passing on orders, throwing tantrums, can you imagine even shouting at those that disobeyed him, was a deeper, manlier thing. This was presumably another way the contradictions inherent in Jackson's complex psychological make-up manifested themselves

– there were the two, or even three, skin colours, the two, or three, sexual placings, or even no sexual shape at all, a sort of sexual less than zero, a gap in the market so to speak, and there was the way his voice could be gentle and yielding when that suited the occasion, and tough and purposeful when that was required. Both voices were used for protection – the weak, heartbroken, boyish one for those moments in mostly televised public when he felt accused and misunderstood, the strong, self-assured grown man one for when he was sorting out business, closing in on a deal, instructing lawyers, or dealing with some friendly rough and tumble. Maybe he used it when he was ordering room service. These alternative voices conveniently reflected the two extremes of his music – the flimsy, vulnerable, pity me ballads, and the hard-on macho don't-underestimate-me frantic dance pop anthems. Or perhaps neither voice was the real thing. Both voices used in certain circumstances hid a real voice, another sound altogether, something known perhaps to so few people no one could honestly describe what it was like, perhaps a voice used when he was in conference with Quincy and his studio team, the normal voice of a normal man of his age and race, one that got used less and less, until Jackson himself lost sight of it, and he was reduced to using the pretend publicity put-upon whimper, or the put-on and purposefully surprising baritone. Perhaps towards the end the only time anyone would ever hear this voice was when he used it, without even knowing he could still use it, to plead with whatever aide or servant or hanger on or medic happened to be nearby to 'help me'.

ELEVEN

The Robsons in particular from the defence point of view are extremely strong witnesses. They come off as honest, reasonable people. (If totally blind to the notion that a normal middle-aged man would not sleep with small boys.) Of the three kids who've said they were molested, two won millions of dollars stemming from the accusations. The third is from a family that's notorious for grifting off celebrities.

TWELVE

The self-described close friends that crawled into position as soon as the switch was pushed that projected Michael into a golden coffin were a morbid collection of eccentric, excitable self-promoters and professional boasters, all of them ultimately superfans to the extent of being stalkers, all of them echoing the narcissistic stress lines, freaky nervous tics, speech impediments and physical peculiarities of their lord and master. They saw many of their own vulnerabilities exhibited in an exaggerated somehow comforting form in the way Jackson dealt with the outside world.

The fired-up freak friends leapt into action as though they had long been preparing for this moment, the moment when they could become apostles of the faith, spread the word, and gratefully draw in some of the glow and power of their mentor, never letting anyone forget that they understood him, supported him, believed in him, loved him. Their job was to protect the memory of Jackson from the damaging, heretic assaults of the suspicious, cynical and ignorant. They faithfully built the halo, and set it into position, so that they could feel secure and holy under its dazzling light.

Perhaps they had been specially selected by Michael all along, as the right kind of insistent, thick-skinned, voluble and undoubting persuader/defenders whose shrill, convinced praise could cut through messy callous media noise and sustain the crackpot, faith-healing edge of Jackson – a long way from the Jackson and Jones team that produced entrancing and relatively radical middle-of-the-road psycho-pop drama – that ultimately had proved the major perpetuating element in the Jackson brand.

The self-important illusionist Uri Geller, the quasi-crazy preacher and activist Al Sharpton and the cynically self-mocking celebrity loon David Gest, all of them with skin, hair and tone clearly derived from the face and fakery of their idol, breathlessly delivered their scripts and well-rehearsed anecdotes. It wasn't clear whether they had last met their master in the past few months, years, decades, how often they were actually in Jackson's company, what they ever talked about: such details were necessarily kept secret in case they gave the game away. You got the feeling that even if they had only ever met Jackson once or twice for a few minutes this promoted them to the standing of friend and confidante – they had got close enough to have made it as an insider, one whose anecdotes about Jackson could marvellously feature the luminous, inscrutable man himself, who, naturally, revealed who he really was only to them.

These supporters could be seen as extreme examples of the kind of loyal, credulous fan that Jackson attracted in what became after all that his declining years, the controversial years, the rotten years, the pathetic years. Now, officially, and more than just a story, The Final Years. The fans of Jackson who stayed loyal in those sorry final years recognised in their troubled but triumphantly famous hero someone who knew more than anyone what it was to be so emotionally and intellectually at sea, who understood the confusion chaste loners and outsiders felt in a world that tended to doubt the feelings of those craving security and solace and attempting to stave off despair in oddball, untraditional ways.

These fans, and the I-alone-knew-the-real-Michael-friend-fans, possess such purity of belief, such devotion, which seems to the cold and judgemental outsider to verge on the hysterical, that at times you wonder if, in honour of the object of their worship, they had feigned a kind of madness, or had actually gone mad – after all, there is a world where Jackson feigned madness because he decided this is what people expected of him, and his whole career for better or worse was based on him giving people what they wanted, what they found intriguing about him, even if it wasn't the music, or the performance. By the end of his life, perhaps the last twenty years, he had decided, as someone who had traditionally always been in control of the choices that were made about how he appear to the public, that he was not expected to act normal. So he would not act normal. He would play up the debauched quirkiness, the withdrawn weirdness, the enfeebled mutant, act out the idea that he was still the poor, unhappy and misunderstood little boy living behind sequined bars at Neverland who needed a normalising mother even after the uncompromising grown-up president of Jackson Inc. had fought to buy the rights to the Beatles songs and vigorously deflected the savage accusations of those that considered him monstrous. This appeared to work – even when there was no music, no songs, or the music didn't quite live up to the lightning flashes of the Quincy Jones-era hits, or the finest Motown fun, he pressed, whirled and schemed his way into our imagination, and stubbornly stayed there. He held over his fans, and the self-justifying media that supplied the fans with all of their information and motivation, the tyranny of a plan, of withheld secrets and staged revelations. He replaced the hit single as a way of impressing upon people his presence and, as far as he was concerned, importance, with a series of regular updates, related to his apparent corruption, or seediness, or innocence, or unorthodoxy, or, quite simply, the fame that had wrapped his fame in more and more fame. His attitude was, if they want me to be mad, I'll show them madness.

His feigned madness then seemed to implode into an authentic madness, or at least an inability to understand that his behaviour was not now seen as the charming, entertaining, dangerously indiscreet but image-strengthening way-out antics of a fantasy pop star living out sweet, juvenile fantasies, an astute subversion of the hurtful wacko image that others had created for him, but an alarming, lurid sign that he had lost sight of reality and of what was appropriate for a middle-aged man to get up to.

For the loyal, unwaveringly devoted fans, and the primitive disciples that Geller, Sharpton and Gest instantly became as though it was their destiny, Jackson represented absolute goodness – and to the sanctimonious outsider this seemed so unlikely that it achieved the quality of a peculiar kind of miracle, or at the very least a dynamically achieved illusion. The more he was accused of unspeakably grubby acts of abuse, the more he actually started to facially adopt the painted, cruel look of a deviant comic-book villain, the more disturbed and disturbing he became, the more the true believers truly believed. To them, he was being maliciously misunderstood by unforgiving forces aggressively keen on removing Michael's special powers. Michael was being lobotomised by this menacing opposition, and therefore the worse, the more frail and helpless he seemed, the more intense the support and companionship, the more he actually needed his fans, which then seemed to multiply how much they needed him.

To the fanatic, overwhelmed by the idea of Jackson as erotic sorcerer, singing mystic and shape-shifting angel of mercy, he, as in He, happened to live in a crude, nasty and suspicious era when such goodness and humility were mercilessly persecuted. It was up to them to explain to the ignorant mob that in fact Jackson was being punished, and actually being ripped apart, not for the alleged acts of molestation, for the loss of originality and magic in his music, for the obsessive, disfiguring cosmetic surgery, for his weakness for the sensational, for the gothic, ritualised ways he organised becoming a father, for the ways his idiosyncratic lifestyle seemed to mock the very standards of decency and fair play he professed to support, for the self-pity, for the stunted development, for the succession of fake marriages and the surrogate mothers, for the ways he seemed convinced his life was only worth living if he could live it as a child. He was being accused and cursed because, through it all, despite his psychic frailties and the constant abuse, he was a pristine, world-changing symbol of hope and love. He was, according to the gospel spread by those who for their own particular reasons saw only resonant purity, threatening not because of his neuroses but because he was so powerfully a proponent of a kind of fragrant, intoxicating positivity. And those that did not love him, or like him, who in fact actively hated him, were simply jealous.

THIRTEEN

What is Michael Jackson according to Google #2

Michael Jackson is known everywhere on the planet
Michael Jackson is the sexiest man alive
Michael Jackson is a ten year old boy trapped in a 49 year old man's body
Michael Jackson is suing British television company Granada
Michael Jackson is the best singer I know of
Michael Jackson proves that many times in life the people that have the least to say end up saying the most through their actions
Michael Jackson is pictured at Exeter City Football Club in Devon on June 14
Michael Jackson is protesting that Sony failed to promote his recent album
Michael Jackson is staging a comeback
Michael Jackson is talking only to himself in an empty universe
Michael Jackson is hitting out at the record industry again
Michael Jackson is as universally known as Coca-Cola

Michael Jackson is Peter Pan

Michael Jackson was the fifth member of Abba

Michael Jackson is where God emptied himself into man

Michael Jackson has yet to reach the climax of his psychodrama

Michael Jackson is in legal combat mode again

Michael Jackson is a freak who abuses children

Michael Jackson is seen outside the high court

Michael Jackson is losing it

Michael Jackson was very pleasant

Michael Jackson is ready to emerge from his debasement

Michael Jackson told Martin Bashir that he allowed kids to sleep in his bed thinking people would think of him as an innocent child but he was very much misunderstood

Michael Jackson's songs were all about how we lose the people we love, we lose our vigour, and we lose our lives

Michael Jackson is my hero contrary to the press about him lately

Michael Jackson is such a gentle man

Michael Jackson has buried his identity

Michael Jackson hangs on the cross forever

Michael Jackson once met Victoria Principal

Michael Jackson 'sang for the famine-stricken of the world as they endured the impotent extremities of starvation' and if that sentence was say the shape of his nose when he was fourteen years old then this sentence 'he had come to realise that there was no deep sense in things, that nothing and no one had real dignity and real deserving, that 'the world' was just a jumble and a rubble and a dream' was the shape of his nose when he was forty four except in fact the nose was now only the size of the word 'rubble.'

Michael Jackson was scheduled to perform 50 sell out concerts to over one million people at London's O2 arena

Michael Jackson is one sick bastard

Michael Jackson is a friend of Shirley Temple

Michael Jackson is a ticking time bomb waiting to explode

Michael Jackson is my best friend

Michael Jackson wore white socks to draw attention to his feet as he danced, feet that fought with all their life against the volatile faithlessness of the human mind

Michael Jackson is hermaphrodite

Michael Jackson doesn't recognise himself

Michael Jackson lives in a dream world but then we all live in dream worlds

Michael Jackson felt the post modern culture revving along inside him

Michael Jackson is oblivious to the protest of Jarvis Cocker

Michael Jackson is knowing what is catchy to a ten year old

Michael Jackson makes sure he is ahead of his time so that his records are played years later

Michael Jackson gazed down on me from above and he had a strangely elongated head and a strange pallor, the pallor of something that had long been deprived of light, a shadowed leaf, a deep sea fish, a grub inside a fruit

Michael Jackson's third child is born in 2002 using his sperm cells with a surrogate mother and an artificial insemination

Michael Jackson is a tourist attraction

Michael Jackson is nobody's memory

Michael Jackson says that men who don't masturbate become kind of unstable

Michael Jackson is destroying his face because he doesn't want to look like his father Joe

Michael Jackson loves you

Michael Jackson is going to duet with Madonna on In The Closet but he doesn't like what she wants to do he think she's too rude

Michael Jackson is taken advantage of because of his money

Michael Jackson is pronounced dead at 2.26 pm local time

Michael Jackson proved that just by being your black self you could make the world yours

Michael Jackson is nicknamed Smelly by Quincy because when Michael liked a groove he'd call it Smelly Jelly and he doesn't curse smelly is his way of saying a bad word

Michael Jackson is singing 'you start to freeze as horror looks you right between the eyes/you're paralyzed'

Michael Jackson is what you could call a health nut

Michael Jackson is in racial and cultural exile

Michael Jackson is like all the rich being victimised as much by his own lawyers and hangers on as he is by those on the outside

Michael Jackson is very much a man and he is very loving and very caring and we never had sex

Michael Jackson is set to a melody as lost and forlorn as an orphaned boy

Michael Jackson is almost running out of money

Michael Jackson is still beautiful

Michael Jackson is speaking in a whisper and wearing a scarf around his throat to protect his golden voice

Michael Jackson's May 1994 marriage to Lisa Marie Presley was short lived and ended in divorce after 2 years

Michael Jackson is a condition that no amount of money can cure

Michael Jackson is writing songs for himself

Michael Jackson would have found his calling with or without his dad he had a God given talent not because he was beaten down by dear old dad

Michael Jackson's face is on the side of a Manhattan bus advertising Invincible just weeks after 9/11

Michael Jackson's defence attorney is pitch perfect

Michael Jackson is overcome by dread

Michael Jackson is the youngest member of the Jackson 5, the embodiment of Motown's claims they were The Sound of Young America and the first black group on the cover of the teen magazine 16

Michael Jackson obtained fertilised eggs from Poland and then had them implanted in Debbie to carry them for him

Michael Jackson is grabbing a water gun and joining in

Michael Jackson is used to coarsened and corrupt public sensibilities

Michael Jackson is making plans to escape

Michael Jackson referred to his young Neverland visitors as 'rubbers' as in something to rub against

Michael Jackson is molesting Gavin only weeks after the Martin Bashir film aired

Michael Jackson is thrusting his pelvis

Michael Jackson is a dolphin

Michael Jackson is spending time talking to dead people

Michael Jackson is having a party

Michael Jackson is the only father they knew and I'm sure he loved them

Michael Jackson is tied down, Gulliver like, by miniature dogs dressed in business suits

Michael Jackson is predicting his own death in 1997 song called Morphine from Blood on the Dance Floor singing 'trust in me/just in me/put all your trust in me/you're doing morphine'

Michael Jackson is dead according to TMZ but his Wikipedia page has not been updated

Michael Jackson is the most hideous thing I have ever seen

Michael Jackson's second bride would be identified as Michael's dermatology nurse Debbie Rowe

Michael is dead from an overdose of propofol which causes a euphoria quite like any other sedative

Michael Jackson is singing 'ain't the pictures enough/ why do you go through so much/to get the story you need/so that you can bury me'

Michael Jackson is scared by the look in his father's eyes

FOURTEEN

When I think about Michael Jackson, I don't think about the music. I don't think about the singing, the dancing, the hits, the videos, the perfectionist craving for some ultimate performance achievement that would embed him into history more comprehensively and unassailably than Chaplin, Astaire, Monroe, Elvis, Hendrix, Brando, the Beatles, Prince.

I wouldn't think about the music immediately, not as something that can totally represent who he was, and what he symbolised and inspired. I cannot just think purely of a brilliant but flawed character easily called by many the greatest entertainer who ever lived – because if he was any such thing, or certainly a resolute contender, then that was because he was so crammed with doubts, paranoia, qualms, phobias and funks, all manner of contradictory energies that spilled over into his entertainment. Ultimately it is the dark, afflicted side of him that actually seemed to eat into his face and mind, the florid self-consciousness increasingly made worse by fame and wealth and all that affectionate and poisonous attention, that fascinates me more than the music.

He thought and felt about himself so unlike anyone else, with such voluptuous narcissism, such obsessive self-destructive commitment to his obsessions, that ultimately it is his mind, his motivation for becoming what he became, his capacity for remaking himself, his convoluted and defensive actions as edgy, diffident and allergic mortal victimised for being so different, that is more interesting than his music. If his pop music had anything special about it, the way it reflected his nerve, fear, impatience, oddness, loneliness, brutalised ordinariness, the scorched, lithe craving of an insecure outsider for love and attention, his desire for the sublime and a way of escaping the fluctuant mess of existence through the needy, often pleading combination of rhythm and consciousness, then it is hard for me to jettison all of that and just hear his songs as songs, as things of value in themselves.

I think of a kind of epic, demonic fantasy as organised by a mischievous, tortured fantasist who was both totally in control of arranging and decorating the fantasy, and completely out of control, beaten into submission by the consequences of the hyperbole, fame and suspicion. A naive, sophisticated fantasist with a monstrous appetite for self-invention who represented through the gloss and allure of expensively constructed and extravagantly distracting commercial entertainment the rapid, disorientating changes in the Americanised world between the late '50s and the early part of the twenty-first century. A surrealist song-and-dance man, who used pop music based on his torrid imagination as a way to invade, and toy with, and trick, our imaginations.

FIFTEEN

Once Michael had ceased to be more musician than mere celebrity, it was the smirking, deadpan media doing the punishing and scapegoating, greedily feeding on his decline, wallowing in his misery, interpreting his eccentricities as a clear sign of criminal behaviour. When he died, they stepped in, naturally, to take charge of how Jackson's image would be decided upon and distributed.

The media, even above friends and family, who could only do so much sustaining their loving memory of Jackson without being able to generate publicity and access, were in the best possible place to take control of how Jackson would be honoured, dishonoured, remembered and buried. The media presented themselves – because they could, they could manipulate it however they wanted – as the force that most understood

Jackson, and, they could maintain, because it was all up to them, that they had the best interests of everyone, fans, family, friends, at heart, and they really took their responsibility seriously in how they presented Jackson to the world.

As a member of the watching, judging media, made up of jostling points of view but somehow always ending up pointing in one direction, did I have any specific position, was there an area of his life where I could be considered an expert? Could I cope with talking about, say, the beautiful boy brilliant Michael Jackson of the Jackson 5 in the post-hippy '70s, this surely incandescent distillation of youthful hope, without considering the disfigured, hunted and arrogant Michael Jackson of the early twenty-first century? Could I smile at the excellently snazzy sight of the innocent but already somehow fictional pre-teenage Michael obediently popularising for teenybop audiences the bewitching urgency of James Brown, the soulful groove of Marvin Gaye, the defiant alertness of Stevie Wonder, the supreme symmetry of Diana Ross, without grimacing at the thought of the disenfranchised and traumatised fifty-year-old Michael, ruined and wiped out because he'd once been this fresh, flashy coquettish pre-teen prodigy, then he was the vivacious, dolled-up, respected czar of MTV, and then, all of a sudden, he wasn't?

And was the older Michael, the exiled wreck, the gruesome light-skinned apparition, the embodiment of agony, some kind of metacultural comment on the existence of the younger, exploited Michael – an explicit warning of some sort, to whoever might be paying attention, that fame is a disease, and that the more intensely it claims you, or you claim it, the more damaging it becomes, the more it breaks up reality and mutilates your soul? That, in fact, to have Jackson's ambition, to want so much to break free of his background, his status and race, to mock ordinariness and limitations, to achieve isolated glory, and therefore to possess his locked-in level of perfectionist fury, can only lead, once reality, and the mundane, actually get in the way, to, if not an early death, then a succession of deaths, a gradual erosion of life, a replacement of one vigorous, visionary being with a wretched, spindly echo.

I tried to think of a situation where I could consider the prematurely soulful, noticeably sorrowful, poignantly trusting lead vocals of the eleven-year-old Michael, the impeccably assembled pop structure of 'I Want You Back', without dealing with the eventual consequences of this early display of commercial ingenuity and enslaved glee – without also appreciating how the young performer would become so spoilt and tormented because he was the nervous, oppressed son of a demanding, dictatorial, bad-tempered father and a fanatically religious, severely controlling mother, working for a series of kind-hearted and/or menacing bosses constantly and possibly aggressively demanding greater levels of precision, charm and sweetness, educating the young performer at such an early age about the ways and means of manipulating a targeted, gullible audience to fall for you, to buy into a fantasy and thus buy the product. To make believe, say, that you are part of a happy, loving, close-knit family when in fact you live in fear of your father and sundry moguls, mercenaries and magnates and find the whole process of performing as though you are having the time of your young life a draining, joyless experience. Fans gasp as you jump for sheer joy surrounded by illumination and loving harmonising brothers but do not understand how you had to get up an hour early this morning to clean the yard and if you failed to do it properly you were beaten with a wire clothes hanger.

He was allowed to experience before he was fourteen the intoxicating, consoling but dubious advantages of being so visibly appreciated and adored for the way you can sing and move and just in a way be. On the one hand he was clearly robbed of what might be considered any kind of normal childhood, and punished for being so fabulously reminiscent of Sammy Davis Jr and Little Stevie Wonder by being forced as a chirpy, well-mannered, clear-eyed little star to fulfil certain paradoxically soul-destroying duties. On the other he was handed various clues how he might achieve through his Motown-framed talents and his well-marshalled exuberance a kind of freedom that went way beyond the potential for independence of the so-called normal teenager.

He had, so the story goes, his childhood snatched away, replaced with hours of regimented practice, he was intimidated, harassed and pressurised into professional routine more or less as soon as he could walk and talk . . .

SIXTEEN

Thousands of fans gathered at a public memorial held at Harlem's Apollo Theater, where a nine-year-old Michael Jackson won an amateur night competition in 1967.

SEVENTEEN

. . . and at the same time was offered tantalising glimpses how he might hang on to his childhood forever – a peculiar personal dream of what childhood actually was, seeing as how he was never allowed any kind of real childhood – because the possible reward for the kind of stardom that was clearly in his grasp is the chance to perpetually postpone the conventional responsibilities of adulthood. By having his childhood erased by the unnatural conditions of being a child star, and therefore achieving a radical sort of non-conformist flexibility, in fact offered the opportunity of a permanent childishness, or at least a chance to recreate throughout his life a version of being young constructed by someone for whom the natural states of being young, the internal fantasies, the chance to play and wish, were mercilessly distorted by those around him using up his precious youthfulness for their own nefarious reasons.

The combination of being controlled by specialist disciplinarians driven by how much business your natural and very serviceable energies could generate, and yet being shown a world where you could actually take control of your own destiny because of a certain kind of mysteriously self-possessed uniqueness, eventually contributed to the way that the bright, bushy-tailed and costumed junior Michael of 'ABC' became, via the imperial, all-conquering, glamorously freakish Michael of 'Billie Jean', the brittle, bitter, defeated and impaired senior Michael that lingered on and on through the '90s and '00s tragically convinced that he could still move, and move us, as though he was a combination of the spinning teen Michael and the thrilling body-blurring and flamboyantly liberated 'Thriller' Michael.

Could I possibly talk about the terrific teen speed of 'Rockin' Robin' and its positive relationship to a very particular history of black showbiz expression and pace-setting African-American showmanship, the all-male singing group with a long noble tradition in both religious and secular fields, without infecting the memory by dwelling on the habitual crotch-grabbing and the baby dangling, the accusations of child molestation, of pain clothed in stylistic clichés and the grandiose self-defensive self-pity that swallowed him up whenever he detected that there was a loss of interest in him, at least as an artist, an entertainer, and not as the ultimate, sinister victim of the frightful insanity of fame?

Can we marvel at the ultimate African-American musician channelling decades of innovative black musical progress – ragtime, jazz, blues, swing, rhythm and blues, rock 'n' roll, soul – into the popular white mainstream by adding his own striving sense of extravagance, mystery and competitiveness without acknowledging that his killer instinct ultimately led to such behavioural strangeness it undermined his achievements? It meant that he can never be taken as seriously as he wanted to be, as an experimental populist rewriting the laws of pop music, continually proving that the popular song could be transcendent and endlessly surprising, because, however stunning his music and performance was, it is always overshadowed by the resultant overwhelming tabloid-weighted weirdness. He was so driven to demonstrate his originality and his ability to stay ahead of the pop crowd, to confound expectations that he ended up pushing his originality too far. His originality shrivelled up into abnormality.

Could I possibly talk about 'Don't Stop 'til You Get Enough' as a shining early example of the supreme collaboration between Jackson and record producer Quincy Jones, who brought to Jackson his sophisticated commercial understanding of how to arrange a piece of music so that a magically balanced coherence could be achieved through the sensitive blending of strings, horns, rhythms, electronics and voice – and the space within all that – without mentioning that once Jackson and Jones stopped working together Jackson was left forever trying to recreate the perfect partnership, and never quite making it? Would that be fair – to deny him a greater part in the history of popular music simply because the artistic and commercial success he attained as he fought free of the child star trap ultimately meant he was perpetually stressed trying to equal that impact, and the pressure became a part of what caused him to crash so horrifically?

Shouldn't it be enough that, with Jones, whom he fought to hire despite the doubts of his record label, who felt Jones was 'too jazz' to add anything to Jackson's already solid record sales, Jackson fulfilled his absurd-seeming ambition to equal the (white, rock) Beatles in making (black, soul) music that was the most technologically advanced, the most culturally charged, and commercially the biggest-selling of all time? If the stupendous effort directly caused the slow, painful descent from grace, shouldn't we excuse, or accept, the catastrophic breakdown as an inevitable consequence of the kind of impact Jackson made, and concentrate simply on the musical and cultural breakthroughs? Remember Jackson as a strutting, stirring, effervescent African-American superhero demonstrating how to succeed in a white American world and a major artistic talent who brought the creative best out of Quincy

Jones, not as a tortured freak behind an eerie mask with seamy private interests, known for once being incredibly well known, who began to believe in himself as some kind of angel of love gifted to the planet in order to save souls and guide humanity forward.

In fact, perhaps we should actively sympathise with the pitiful, hounded Jackson, who gave so much to realise his fantasy of success and domination that it destroyed him, as if he sacrificed himself simply so that in an increasingly complicated, demanding and cynical world he could still produce the kind of internationally recognised superstardom that officially ranked with Elvis and the Beatles. He became unbelievably pathetic, embarrassing and even obnoxious, but wasn't that simply the ultimate fate of someone who climbed so high, while so in the spotlight, and was so exceptionally rewarded? That much fame cannot be easily processed, especially by someone who never really had any fully formed memory of what it was like not to be famous.

Of course, even to concentrate on the irresistible fast-moving finger-snapping pop delights of 'ABC' is to ignore the mushy, maudlin side of the young Jackson, or at least that pre-teen girl-pleasing schmaltzy side of Jackson as coordinated by his prudent manufacturing masters and arrangers combined with his own arrested instincts for pleasing hormonally agitated young people who identified with his touching expressions of hurt, confusion and lovesickness.

He was singing 'I'll Be There' and 'Ben', and as much as he would pursue the wild dream of blending ethereal black soul passion with macho white rock attack on his best-loved hits, concerned we might consider him too wimpy if there was no such zeal, he never shook off this commitment to the affected, simpering ballad. There was the crotch grabbing, the scrupulous attention to dance rhythm detail, the buying in of hard rock guitar heroes for regular doses of mock mayhem, and the constant need to capture in compromised form newly generated urban energies. Always, though, a need for softness, for wrapping himself and all of the world in a blanket of love and affection, where there is no danger, and no angry, possibly violent parental intrusion – where, presumably, there could be some gentle crotch stroking and a mound of mooching.

For Jackson, the airy, tender, pious ballads were another way of tapping into the otherworldly areas where he ended up feeling most at home, and he never freed himself of this early part of the formula – in fact, the gushing sentimentality and epic gentleness metastasised just as much as any other part of the Jackson make-up that was established in those early years, when he was living out a childhood enjoying and consuming pop culture not simply as a fan but actually himself as a pop culture ingredient. (This led to the middle-aged Jackson that was hysterically, and in a way courageously, clinging on to his responsibility as pop culture icon while at the same time basing all his experiences of reality on an imaginative world consisting almost completely of pop culture references. He was never able to escape the idea that the world was a cartoon because in a way from his earliest time as a performer and kid he was already a kind of cartoon himself, literally so in the silly, colour-drenched, kid-friendly Saturday-morning Jackson 5 cartoon series that placed him in the early 1970s squarely in a world of Bugs Bunny and Peter Pan. The boys were always getting in and out of trouble! And at the end of each frantic episode, of course, once everything had been sorted out, a song, a minor, or major, Motown marvel. He felt that he was able to do things to himself and the world around him that you could only do in a cartoon.

In a cartoon, nothing he did to himself, nothing he did to his body, nothing he believed about his own powers, his ability to change the world, to change his race, to change people's minds, to create fantasies around him, to defy gravity, the most unreasonable demands, the most extraordinary moves he made as his body snapped, melted or morphed from one shape to another, whether because of sense of rhythm or intrusive surgery, none of this would have been beyond the realms of possibility. He lived his life, perhaps, following principles established in cartoons, where reality could be bent to your will, there were no germs, no sign of voice-spoiling pollution, and there were no limits to your appearance, and your powers, and the emotional or physical violence you might cause yourself or others, without ever really causing permanent harm. In a cartoon, you were free, to experiment with your shape, colour and size, to manipulate the details of any contact you may have with others, to touch the sky and freeze time, to dress up as dramatically as you wanted, to talk to the animals, to avoid questions of sex – what is more sexless than a cartoon, where reproduction never requires messy, mysterious intercourse? – and to continually re-imagine your environment. In a cartoon, you can be whoever you want to be, you can glide across the surface of the moon, you can segue from zombie dance routine to a super-sterile space station, you can star with Marlon Brando and Eddie Murphy. You can save the entire human race, earn and spend fabulous fortunes, and you never grow old, and all adventures, however scary and intimidating, can be made to lead to a happy ending, and then it starts again, as if you are born again, and ready for anything. You could be whoever you wanted to be and who was going to stop you?)

To just talk about the animated, elated Jackson 5 Michael, the cute whirlwind topped off with an adorable mini-afro deliciously hinting at the far less tamed and far more threatening forces of black power, is to be selective, to ignore the soft-centred, gooey songs he sung that more blatantly exposed the idea that the group was cynically set up to be a mainstream pop phenomenon. This is the thing with Michael Jackson. You can choose what you wish to celebrate, or praise: the cultural maverick who smashed through early '80s racial barriers on the white, rockist MTV, the astonishing dancer who catapulted Astaire, Kelly and Nureyev into the shrieking pop future, the postmodern bandleader who coordinated the creation and imagery of a series of lavish set pieces that helped transform him into a video age living legend and a major internet era topic of conversation – but can you ignore the oddness, accusations and martyred sourness, the compulsion to entertain by so explosively displaying his psychic wounds? You can dwell on the curious and the perverse, the man whose megalomania was a front for a great deal of misery, the whitewashed dynamo who burnt himself out by the age of thirty with ankles that resembled his wrists, the putrefying hyperstar leaking the odour of decomposition into the late twentieth century, but can you reject the restless American genius and his sincere assertion that 'human capacities have no limits'?

I waited for the calls to come, and wondered what my take would be. Should be. Could be. What did I believe? Which Michael Jackson did I believe in? Was it possible to believe in only one Michael Jackson? How many Michael Jacksons were there, how many macabre permutations, how many commercial envoys?

Actually, did I believe at all in a Michael Jackson that

was in control of a Michael Jackson, or was the thing I believed in not Jackson himself, the fascinating music, the shattered image, the reclusive spookiness, the convoluted history, but the response to Jackson, the coverage and interpretation of the different periods of his life, the speculation about his defects, and drive, and addictions, and self-abuse, that ended up, or could not possibly end up, with a single all-encompassing idea of who he actually was and what he really represented?

Did I believe only in the creation of Michael Jackson by an entertainment media – therefore by the end of Jackson's life, just about all of the media, and the emergence of new forms of media created by the internet that favoured the rejection of considered, contextualised analysis of events, trends and circumstances – and the voyeuristic consumers of the media? Was the Michael Jackson I found myself thinking about an invention of the media – and therefore in fact the media itself, the media in human form?

The media had itself during Jackson's lifetime become so fascinated with sexual crimes and pornographic details of those crimes, and with sex, and money, and image, and fame, and wide-eyed, attractive young singers of gut-wrenching ballads and gutted electro-rock, and the myth of eternal youth, the obsession with physical appearance, and celebrity humiliation, and celebrity surgical transformation, with celebrities being increasingly positioned as role models, that the '80s Jackson seemed ultimately like an avant-garde experimental anticipation of this new world. Jackson set up a world where the stories that most people were exposed to, and learnt to love, and feed off, were the petty details of some life or another of someone famous for a while or famous for the famous fifteen minutes, a life pulverised by newspaper and gossip magazine headlines. Jackson invented in his detached, histrionic image the mock-world of late-twentieth-century celebrity gossip, where reality started to be eaten up by reality TV, which then started to take over the twenty-first century to the point where the kinky, artificial and fanciful took over the reality of the world.

A world where face lifts, nose jobs, liposuction, breast enlargements, cheek implants, tattooed eyebrows, hair straightening and botox were now normal, everyday, actually desirable things, and the idea of the flaws, fights, failures and trivial fuck-ups of styled, sponsored, willingly exploited celebrity freaks being monitored daily by a wacko media and its wacko clients and customers using skilfully engineered music and recycled fashion as forms of reality controlling stimulation and sedation was no longer some dystopian science fiction fantasy.

Was this Jackson I did believe in actually the spirit of the age – perhaps the cause, through no fault of his own, or maybe it was entirely his fault, because he couldn't cope with being the son of a tyrant, and he was so famous it actually really did hurt, and so seduced by a fantasy of wealth – of this neurotic, nervy, self-ish, scandalous world made up of commercially organised, manipulated and titillating image and its constant seductive soundtrack? Michael Jackson's legacy did not lie in a vibrant transference of the militant, soulful, persecuted, spirited energies of his mentors with their active inner lives and their rampaging sensuality, but inside the tatty, lurid details of the Katie Price/Peter Andre divorce, inside Simon Cowell's love for triumphalist kitsch and money-generating excess.

This was his influence – as the king of wannabes. As the king of the self-invented minor celebrity. As the king of surgically enhanced frivolity. As the king of the emotional emptiness of modern, Godless humanity who were either trapped by shopping or refused the freedom to shop.

The king of this superficial distillation of pop's cosmopolitan stimulations because of how he looked stitched together out of copied bits of his favourite stars and singers: his identification with the untouchable glamour of stars as framed, filtered and made permanent through film, TV, video; how he behaved, as though it was all about him; the twisted, sentimentalised guilt about the abstractly felt sufferings of others; the excuses he could dredge up to explain his errant behaviour; the way he accumulated great wealth and then indiscriminately spent it; the way he craved a perpetual adolescence where he could play games, party, and have what he wanted; his belief that dancing to brilliantly manufactured electronic pop music could lead to a blissful escape from life's mundane pressures; the sense you got that he never read a book – and if he did, he hid it, because such a thought would alienate regimented post-modern consumers dismissive of any literary ways of expressing, savouring and defining the imagination; the way he represented his fascination with horror and the dark side through hypnotic special-effect spectacle as though this way he could control chaos; the endless ways he transformed himself inside his entertainment zones from cute boy to ghoul, mystic to hooligan, human to animal, pursuing a mutable identity; the strong recommendation he handed on to successive generations that you could break out of a grim working-class background and associated horrors through the power of song and dance, that all problems could be solved by passing an audition, and impressing a select few judges, and powering to glory.

There were also, of course, the ways he regularly altered his appearance as if by doing so he could first of all achieve the dream of everlasting youth and secondly outwit death, and even when he did die, in the middle of an induced sleep that was perhaps even deeper than death, he had by then ensured he would never be forgotten . . . He had, what with one thing and another, succeeded at never being forgotten. Because he was different, and everything he had done to himself was because he had to maintain that difference as everyone started to catch up with just how different he started out being.

No one could now ever forget him, not, perhaps, because of his singing and dancing, but because of the spectacle he made of himself, sustaining his 'difference' through a grandiose collection of gimmicks, publicity tricks, uniforms, silly rumours, gallivanting and delusional pomposity.

His exploits as hero and villain had directly inspired this hollow, self-indulgent pop struck world, one that had slowly taken over even the mainstream news, whether the majority of people wanted it, most surely not as caught up in the machinations of pop culture as the entertainment industry and those invested in its success. He did this by first being commercially fascinating and relishing the hard-edged suspense he could create through song and dance, and then by simply recreating his level of fame by replacing music and imaginative effort with stunts, so that the product that promoted him was not his music and records, produced with the same kind of commitment and self-awareness that led to *Off the Wall* and *Thriller*, but the scandals, the court cases, mysterious illnesses, the paternity suits, the pet chimps, the television documentaries and interviews, the big-budget greatest hit campaigns, the masks, the whitening of the skin, the rumours of various absurd alliances.

This was also Jackson's legacy – not so much passing

forward the lessons, vocals and style he had inherited from Tharpe, Wonder, Gaye, Robinson, Ross, Astaire and Cagney but creating a world where pop stars would essentially merely be selling themselves and their bland, branded mega-image, with the music a kind of tightly controlled, highly formularised, technically neat side-product. In his later years, after all, he was more influenced by the death of Diana as a major historical landmark and the relentlessly photographed flaunting of an expensively empty but ever present Paris Hilton as a demonstration of cultural importance than by anything musical. (In this sense you could see how he was the missing link between the elegant, troubled Marvin Gaye and the boorish, aggrieved Kanye West, and a major signpost on an entertainment road to ruin that replaced a certain sort of sonically represented social consciousness and emotional sensitivity with a plain and simple sonic representation of boasting, preening and coasting. He played a vital role in directing a long, courageous history of dissident black music towards it being smothered in capitalist drag.)

By the end of Michael Jackson's life, he was us, reflecting back at us the insatiable, submissive way we now consume pop culture, showing us what the ultimate end can be of a life obsessed with putting on a public face, with permanent play, stymied by arrested development and a complete indifference towards a world that isn't dedicated to pleasure and dressing up. If somehow, as a well-regulated apparently discriminating collective of consumers and customers and media addicts, we looked in a mirror to check the recent adjustments to our appearance we would see the ravaged, savaged bashed-in ashen faceless face of Michael Jackson staring back at us. The mirror would then point out, this being a Jackson-based fantasy, that we were still the fairest of them all. And we would believe it.

And when he died, because he had helped create the environment, a flash, tabloid-shaped, app-saturated, ring-toned, Google-searched, Twitter-reduced, sensation-seeking, gossip-boggled world of Paris Hilton and Amy Winehouse, Kanye West and Taylor Swift, Justin and Britney, Mary-Kate and Ashley Olsen, Jessica and Ashlee, Beyoncé and Jay-Z, Rihanna and Chris, *X Factor* and *American Idol*, E! and TMZ, Cowell and Seacrest, Gaga and Pattison, a world where commercial success was increasingly made the only official sign of creative quality, a certified classic song only one that went platinum, he was not slipped into an aside as simply a famous pop singer from the MTV age dying (shame, weird guy though) and moving on: the requirement was to celebrate him, as something awesome and influential, with any flaws and defects attributed to his unassailable genius.

He had helped build a youth-conscious media world that was now guaranteed to hail the sad passing of an extravagantly eccentric entertainment guru as though it

was in fact an event that contained genuine spiritual qualities that marked a significant cultural moment. He had
ensured by accident and design that the media followed
his methods of faking reality for their own commercial
ends, and therefore, when he died, they effortlessly faked
a situation where Michael Jackson was more important
than being just an impressive genre-fusing crowd-pleaser
who sold a lot of records and won awards and worked
out how to play MTV at their own game and made a bit
of a hash of dealing with the impact on his tense nervous
system of some personal difficulties and an amount of
fame that got out of hand. He was in fact, even though it
was all a fiction massaged into shape over a few decades,
genuinely a special, important royal king with unique
compassion who had died before his time.

No comment on how he had been pushed to replace
himself with someone, something, else, persuaded to try
and become what he was clearly never meant to be –
white, wholesome, sexually conventional, heterosexual,
a father – in order to satisfy the no-nonsense conventional demands of narrow-minded, intolerant American
public opinion. The barely there ex-pure electroghost
that trailed slime, debt and defeated loopiness around
the edges of the entertainment world long after it had
reached what was probably the natural end of its life
had become so distorted and wretched not least because
it had been encouraged to think that if it was white and
part of a family, it would be accepted. These edges of

the entertainment world that would once have been very rarely checked out could now, because of the internet, the entertainment shows that had built up to fulfil the demand for infantile information about celebrities with something to promote and the rapacious twenty-four-hour news channels, be propelled right into the centre of everything. Entertainment took over, confirming there was no such thing as reality, only a collective madness. This suited Jackson, the major star of the well-remembered '80s who had never quite reclaimed his position as fully functioning superstar making the hottest, smartest high street records of the day, was also operating in a dingy twilight zone of intrigue that positioned him at the level of a busted minor celebrity. Somewhere between Pamela Anderson and David Hasselhoff, one who might get a reality show on a camp channel following his every distinctively erratic move and sniggering at his hilarious, hopeless, possibly pernicious relationship with his children.

When the two sides, the historical pop icon and the trashy reality star, collided, as they sometimes did, there could still be a close reminder of just how potent a presence he was, if not much of a reminder of what it was like to hear the 'Thriller' bass materialise for the first few times, as though it was giving us some radiant clue to how Michael Jackson actually perceived the world – as if he had said a few words to Quincy, about his hopes, fears and aching need for something he couldn't quite work out how to resolve, dropped in a few fugitive images, explained yet again about the other dimension he could reach when he sang, about how it helped him emerge out of the crushing dark and into the smashing light, and Quincy had conspired to come up with this giant-sized warning sound, which captured in its swanky, insouciant attack and intricate machine-maintained minimalism, its delirious sureness, Jackson's fierce anxiety, disordered confidence and perversely nerveless determination.

If you really wanted to get to some kind of truth about Michael Jackson, then somehow you would need to interview the sound of that bass, which would be able to answer with some stunning revelations about Michael's early memories, the enigmatic traumas he suffered, his need to order the world around him through the kind of fantasy songs he was now singing, the way he responded to the right sound as though it was a magic potion that could lift him out of his past, and his present, how he ended up so self-demanding, and it was his way of counterpunching, fighting back against the dark, against his shyness, and the doubters, and sometimes the biggest doubter of all was him, never sure he could be as good as he needed to be, to have such a spunky sound, underpinning such a song, built in the image of his trembling, surging imagination and calculated to reflect right into the eyes of those looking towards him his superabundant nervous energy.

EIGHTEEN

Posted by jon at June 30, 2009-09-20:

'I think Michael was more talented at ten years old than most everyone else (who was not a Beatle) at age fifty. It appears he was abused, and the Jehovah's Witness teaching will hammer any child. Also it appears that he had the emotional level of a child. Not withstanding his hyper sexual/danced music and lyrics. He couldn't kiss his wife in public, its sad. Jesus knows us better than we know ourselves. I am inclined to believe Michael loves Jesus. But I am only someone who never met him. I am sad that he was not able to show what he was capable of in his comeback concert series. No one knows if he will be breathing tomorrow. Michael is now in the hands of our saviour. May God rest his soul.'

NINETEEN

No reflection in the immediate post-death news coverage on the particular timing of his major success, during the early Reagan years, where his poised and polished, and extremely expensive, sound, was sexed-up funk, lavish soul and original hardcore disco diligently diluted and expertly modified in order to reach the fussy, prejudiced white audience – a black performer introducing white elements into black music as the opposite of Presley more or less kicking this whole dream/nightmare off as a white performer introducing black elements into white music.

Could I say this kind of thing in a radio interview, or on a television show, in the hours after his death, restrict myself to examining how he failed to make the move from immaturity to maturity, plunge into his inner self and examine how it didn't exist, not in ways we can ever fully understand, and remark on the ways the media created the monster, and then dwelt on it, spurned it, fed it, starved it, tortured it, operated on it, killed it? Could I make the point, at a time when we are all more focused than usual on what Michael Jackson really meant, that he was a burnt-out symbol of ourselves and our indulgences, when perhaps all that was wanted was a brief, genial, if slightly guarded comment that Michael was gentle and kind but a notorious perfectionist and intensely dedicated to his craft?

And was it too much to talk about his excessive precocity as a gifted eleven-year-old forced to perform on demand, how he leapt free of his own teenage history, the ominous intensity and biographical melodrama of the beautifully produced 'Billie Jean', how the original title of the Rodney Temperton song 'Rock with You' was 'Eat You Up', his ability to make music that mixed the kitsch and the transcendent, the flow and tension of his dancing, how the title track of *Off the Wall* when his life and career could still follow improvised paths revealed some kind of manifesto relating to his haywire life and polluted innocence – 'the world is on your shoulder | life ain't so bad at all | if you live it off the wall' – and how if you're looking for the truth about why he ended up the way he ended up, the perfect figure to play Edgar Allen Poe in a movie, then listen to his song 'Childhood'– 'before you judge me | try hard to love me | the painful youth I've had'.

TWENTY

Someone asks me if I like Michael Jackson. Now there's a question. And if I like Michael Jackson, what is it, exactly, that I am liking? It seems like a very simple question, and I imagine there are some people who can answer the question very quickly, and emphatically, and with a fair amount of satisfying completeness, without thinking about it too much. They do not find the question particularly troubling. They know what it is to like, or not like, Michael Jackson, and instantly imagine a Michael Jackson, a moment, a memory, a thing, a hook, one thing, one person, singing one song, 'Rock with You', say, that snare drum at the start, snapping you to attention, a descendant of 'Like a Rolling Stone' wearing roller-skates, one person, on the cover of one record, part of a cartoon series, singing about a rat, a favourite period, *Off the Wall*, say, more gritty, less theatrical than *Thriller*, one person, having hits at eleven years old, it's just about 1970, so much enthusiasm and radiance trapped in song, one person, part of the Jackson 5, beyond a boy band but all that a boy band could ever be, one person, when he was sexy, or something dangerously close, when he was writing songs that sonically explored the idea of sex, in a way perhaps he never physically did, so that the songs he wrote or sang when he was just about twenty and then for a few years were pop as sex, fame as lust, sound as foreplay, rhythm as release, one person, introducing his moon-walk at the twenty-fifth anniversary of Motown, before he was strange, really strange, or was he always stranger, because he was a stranger to himself, moving in public as if such motion solved everything, one person, when he was young and good-looking, really good-looking, one person, singing that the kid is not my son, and the guitar catching up with his thinking, one person, singing another song, 'Beat It', say, the carefree way he presents himself as some kind of warrior with the intention of somehow letting his younger, enslaved self know that everything was going to turn out all right, he was giving himself back, body and soul, to the poor unhappy and misunderstood boy who needed him, giving that young boy the strength, in fact, to ensure that he ends up with the kind of life-loving self-confidence that means he can end up writing and performing and starring in a song as sure, aroused and ecstatic as this, so that 'Beat It' is somehow a gift to his younger self, a rescue plan, a light at the end of the tunnel.

So some people can be asked the question, do you like Michael Jackson, and the answer is obvious, they know where they stand, it was all about the music, he is only the music, and the good times, and the bravado, and the brilliance, and nothing can take away the solvent shrewdness and ecstatic joy, and calls for the metaphorical lynching are unfair, if not actually evil. The music is all we can know; everything else is just total conjecture, unreliable biography, prejudiced speculation, vicious teasing that has got nothing to do with the pure evidence of the singing and the dancing.

Do I like Michael Jackson? That makes me think. Was I ever a fan? Did I ever actually buy a Michael Jackson record? Did I ever really get it out of my head that Michael Jackson was nothing more than the black Donny Osmond – this is something the self-styled American dean of rock critics Robert Christgau got out of his system in 1973, when rock writers had really started to take control of the history, not losing their place for a couple of decades or so, noting that for all the 'sweetness and cleanness' here was a 'real interpreter'.

For me, there was always the Donny thing, even as Michael grew up, and began to swerve and swivel through the changes that would never actually stop, until he at last had to stop, because he died, as he went about shaking off the innocence, the lightweight childishness, if not the sweetness, of those early years, as he worked on the greatest relationship of his life, with Quincy Jones, and most vividly expressed all the struggles and contradictions that flooded his sensibility. In fact, even during the Quincy era, when the patience and experience, the general, technical and conceptual musical wisdom and structural insight of Jones coincided so perfectly with Jackson's private and public yearnings and a series of major cultural and technological shifts in emphasis, the resulting blockbuster music still seemed to be more about sales figures and the accumulation of wealth. Youthful playfulness had merely been replaced with professionally calibrated storytelling that isolated and emphasised brilliantly spotted trends in dance pop music and followed very closely recommendations on how to proceed with the soundtrack to the life of Michael Jackson taken from the results of some market research.

To me, it was still a Donny thing, the creation and marketing of mundanely enterprising light entertainment, however conscientiously motivated, however sensitive it was to the musical movements and efforts of more original talents – and if Michael Jackson was the Michael Jackson to the Donny Osmond of Donny Osmond, then even at his most renowned and record-breaking, even as the 'Thriller' video lifted him on to the top of a world packed with fans whose hearts he'd made race faster, even as he crossed over into a whole new state of MTV being, Michael Jackson seemed the Donny Osmond to the Prince of Prince. The whole thing seemed somehow a mathematical certainty, the inevitable end result of a series of boardroom calculations, investigations, budgets, hunches and decisions.

To some extent, as musical as the whole organisation of Quincy Jones was, as in the team he built and the way he approached the architecture of the music, his marvellous assembly of musicians, engineers, tone, style, technology to help fully realise a fantasy of what Michael Jackson's music should sound like, it didn't touch me as a mainly musical thing. It struck me as being the meticulously designed soundtrack to the far-fetched life of Michael Jackson, a life that was being played out like a movie, and in that sense *Off the Wall*, but especially *Thriller*, and then the final Jones album *Bad*, these increasingly industrial constructions, followed increasingly strict notions of what kind of mock dissident, pseudo-spiritual, neo-wanton, tautly plausible music the biggest pop music superstar in the world should sing. But then I was thinking like a rock critic, threatened with extinction, or at least an almost forgotten place in history.

TWENTY-ONE

What is Michael Jackson according to Google #3

Michael Jackson is intoxicated by his own talent and ability
Michael Jackson enjoys extravagant shopping sprees
Michael Jackson is very cool
Michael Jackson is a licensing agreement
Michael Jackson is saying I am just like everyone else I

cut and bleed and I'm easily embarrassed

Michael Jackson turned up for his courthouse appearance more than an hour late in pyjama bottoms, slippers and a suit jacket

Michael Jackson no longer has to experience mundane life

Michael Jackson drinks wine hidden in a soda can

Michael Jackson is the next Elvis

Michael Jackson fell in the toilet and couldn't get out

Michael Jackson's performance was enough for the world but it was never enough for him

Michael Jackson is showing the writer Danny Fields who went on to manage the Ramones a studded vest he had stitched himself and he wondered whether Danny liked it or thought it 'too busy'

Michael Jackson is willingly making his soul available for commodification

Michael Jackson is singing and crying at the end of She's Out of My Life written by Tom Bahler an ex boyfriend of Karen Carpenter who left him after she found out he had another life as a married man and father

Michael Jackson is outside the constraints of normal human behaviour

Michael Jackson is destined to be ripped apart by an angry crowd

Michael Jackson is diverting public attention from genuinely pressing issues

Michael Jackson can bring with him into a room such moroseness and then manufacture such crazy revelry on stage

Michael Jackson is saying I love fairy tales. I like fantasy a lot, science fiction. I like magic. I like to create magic. I love magic

Michael Jackson and Farrah Fawcett Majors versus Elvis Presley and Groucho Marx

Michael Jackson self crowned like Napoleon is surrounded by cheering, hysterical crowds

Michael Jackson was relentless in his quest to help others

Michael Jackson is singing 'there's no need to dismay/ close your eyes and drift away'

Michael Jackson is moving effortlessly from quiet to loud

Michael Jackson tried to push Judy Garland off the yellow brick road

Michael Jackson is not changing his behavior after being charged with sexual molestation of a 13 year old cancer survivor

Michael Jackson hiccoughs in the middle of songs

Michael Jackson is sent to sleep using propofol which can induce priapism in some people

Michael Jackson's edition of Robinson Crusoe was an edition published in 1887 by Estes and Lauriat of Boston

Michael Jackson was Mike to Akon who tried to tell him he didn't always have to be ahead of the pack he should just stick to what made him great in the first place with an added bit of whatever the newest technology was

Michael Jackson is wandering admiringly through a shrine to Elizabeth Taylor

Michael Jackson was going to sing Bad with Prince but Prince said it 'would be a hit without me' so he didn't do it

Michael Jackson gets the blood going

Michael Jackson is walking into a room totally naked with a hard on and the brothers were totally grossed out

Michael Jackson is increasing circulation

Michael Jackson's face is on a $20 bill

Michael Jackson didn't find it easy to smile

Michael Jackson's smile is twisted in agony

Michael Jackson doesn't know if he was his father's golden child

Michael Jackson is confronting rumours about his skin colour

Michael Jackson is still grabbing his crotch

Michael Jackson is forgiven because he is show business

Michael Jackson cannot be rescued by his personal physician

Michael Jackson is moving to Bahrain so is a muslim

Michael Jackson is doubting everything in the world

Michael Jackson craves information about freaks of nature

Michael Jackson is a modern day crucifixion

Michael Jackson did bleach his skin they found the skin bleaching ointments in his home

Michael Jackson is playing 50 shows at the O2 Arena because Prince played a month long season there and he wants to out do him

Michael Jackson obviously needs psychological help

Michael Jackson's death is causing web-traffic havoc

Michael Jackson is using the Beatles songs to stave off debt

Michael Jackson is singing 'it doesn't matter who's right or wrong'

Michael Jackson is talking about his belief in God with Geraldo Rivera

Michael Jackson would have to be invented if he didn't exist

Michael Jackson is being scammed

Michael Jackson's top half looks like the male of the praying mantis whose upper part has been half devoured by the female but who perseveres in his copulation

Michael Jackson appeared on the Larry King show as Dave the day of his burial

Michael Jackson smiles like a lizard

Michael Jackson is reflecting the contemporary cultural struggle to be both hyper-sexual and innocent, to be true to ones roots while trying to make it and assimilate

Michael Jackson will die before the abuse trial ends fears his former spiritual advisor Rabbi Shmuley Boteach

Michael Jackson is the son of a crane operator at a steel mill

Michael Jackson is a puppet made of wood come to life

Michael Jackson is eaten by Free Willy

Michael Jackson had two children with Debbie Rowie, Prince Michael and Paris Katherine Michael

Michael Jackson CD prices are going up in second hand shops

Michael Jackson is cooing in the middle of his songs

Michael Jackson is trapped in an endless web of make believe

Michael Jackson is a sad sight emerging from his Neverland Valley

Michael Jackson is a space alien drag queen

Michael Jackson as a Jehovah witness child is forbidden from celebrating Christmas and now has Christmas decorations hanging up in June

Michael Jackson is ending the song with an angel coming down to hug and embrace him

Michael Jackson's self-destruction is one of our modern entertainment luxuries

Michael Jackson ached with the need to convince himself that he did exist in the real world

Michael Jackson is a believer in the hopeful impulse that makes beginnings and seeks outcomes and imagines adventures in the middle

Michael Jackson is maintaining that sharing his bed
    with children is an entirely innocent expression of
    affection

Michael Jackson is addicted to tranquilisers, painkillers
    and alcohol

Michael Jackson was not breathing

Michael Jackson's father said his father treated him the
    same way and he thought it was ok because he was
    raised like that

Then for Michael Jackson time stopped.

TWENTY-TWO

A first call came, within an hour of the extremely distracting death bulletin, for some sort of comment, on
some late-night radio show, with – under the circumstances I found myself in, not sure I really had anything
precise enough to say about Michael Jackson – the
worst possible brief. The one where you are innocently
asked to 'sum up his career', no doubt in three minutes,
by some poor assistant producer following hastily issued
orders from above rifling through numbers of pop journalists hoping for some kind of response from anybody
they can get hold of.

    I'd been watching the television news channels catch
up with the idea of a dead and done Michael Jackson. The timing of his death coincided with many pop
journalists and entertainment correspondents camping
out at the Glastonbury pop festival. To those that put

together news shows, this must have seemed a very lucky break, that the right kind of interviewers and experts were located together where there were handy outside broadcast units all ready to beam back early responses. Surely it was all pop music, and Glastonbury was pop music, and the two things, the festival and the death, were therefore a perfect fit, as if one would become a natural stage for the Lennon-like, Diana-deep grief that was surely going to rage through the pop world.

It wasn't really the same thing at all. In fact it would have been more useful to have had an audience comment on his death at the Wimbledon tennis championship happening at the time, a Milton Keynes nightclub or a matinee of the *Dirty Dancing* musical, because in fact the idea of Glastonbury represented much about the music business that had frustrated Jackson in his quest to be accepted as a major artistic talent – filled with the kind of alternative music, rooted in punk, and grunge, and a more artsy, and very white, risk-free rock attitude, give or take a safe, sanctioned token flash of rap and soul, that to him remotely represented something very unexciting and cynical. This was a world that could somehow mock the kind of commercial success Jackson was the ultimate, horrendous example of while simultaneously hoping for it as well, and if they got it, enjoying it in their own way as much as Jackson.

Glastonbury appeared to gently represent diversity, positive communal spirit and easygoing open-mindedness, but it was as much a reflection of the vast, controlling entertainment industry of music, the devious pursuit of a shrewdly targeted youth and post-youth audience following specific trends, as anything that Jackson had been involved with. In a way, with its roots in a very white late '60s hippy world, and with a sensibility updated into a predominantly white and anti-theatrical post-punk alternative universe, it was a reminder of the dogmatic rock attitudes of the early MTV, of the kind of early '80s commercially and culturally convenient if ultimately impractical racial barrier that Jackson and Jones were so determined to break down.

It was a reminder of the early '90s, when Jackson was under the stress of his fame and a new mammoth deal with Sony, not to seem passé. He was searching for a harder, meaner, post-superstar, post-Quincy, post-rap, post-house style he could again call his own, releasing *Dangerous*, working hard to reframe his now standard intensity, sweetness, moodiness and volcanic self-consciousness inside a musical hybrid that didn't leave him stuck in the '80s – he'd made the jump from the '70s to the '80s, but that was from the basis of being a medium-sized superstar. His leap into the '90s was from the position of huge superstardom, which made the move harder not easier, and also he was operating in a groove-fixated dance pop context that was many genres and sub-genres moved on from where it had been with 1982's *Thriller* and even 1987's *Bad*. Through sheer will, the hiring of Prince-conscious, Quincy-respecting, hybrid beat master Teddy Riley as main producer, his enduring competitive fight now transferring into a deeper neurotic fear that he was being left behind as pop star and innovator, he managed to ensure that *Dangerous*, while not as hook heavenly as *Off the Wall*, or *Thriller*, not quite as much an event as *Bad*, was not at all a disaster.

The trouble was, even as Michael proved, again against odds dramatically stacked against him, that he could get on not only without his father, his brothers, or Gordy, or Gamble and Huff, or, most impressively, without Quincy, that he could extend and modernise lessons learnt back at Motown, and then through Philly, and maestro Jones, the pop world's attention was not as such completely interested in a regenerated Michael Jackson. Nirvana, much more of a Glastonbury model of where pop currents swirl around a zeitgeist, more comfortable to a rockist mentality, were of the moment, and Michael was just another star from the as yet not romanticised and recycled pop past fighting to adapt to an increasingly fast-changing, now very much CD-shaped pop world. Such natural results of pop's natural need to replace itself with another version of itself in order to maintain the illusion that it was still alive with future-fancying possibility did not help Michael's frustrations.

There had been many changes in pop because Michael and Quincy worked out how to crash into the opaque MTV building: many more black superstars liberated by

Jackson's success and able to create exotic fantasies of glamour and wealth inspired by Jacksonic principles, and many new trends replacing old trends and then in turn being replaced themselves. In many ways, though, not a lot had changed since Jackson's peak imperial phase.

The pirouetting pop of spectacle and gossip that Jackson had set in motion had not led to the kind of music featured at Glastonbury, even in the dance tents, and even when it was acting a little camp and playful and inviting 'surprise' guests like Kylie or the Pet Shop Boys. Jackson pop, linked through thick and thin, across whatever commercial cosmetic surgery and studio revision, to the evangelical fervour and fire-breathing preachers of the rural south, had led – with a little penetrating nudge from his carnal show business fad-following stepsister Madonna and a generous hit of swanky hip hop smarts, both of which were themselves in debt to the luxury sight of the mighty shamanic Michael conquering the world by setting himself inside an illusion of his own mercurial making – to Xtina, Britney, Justin, Kanye, Rihanna, to Whitney, Mariah and Leona. From a dogmatic rock perspective, Jackson pop was vulgar, vaudevillian, aristocratically minded, utterly reliant on visual imagery, based on an adoration of traditional Hollywood, and, for all the black-and-blue lusting and thrusting, ultimately committed to a certain sort of domestic, conformist sleekness. It was best heard and seen set inside a television studio, a darkened club or an indoor arena. It was not very open air. It was not at all the elite, progressive pop of Glastonbury. Only death could bring Jackson in any kind of contact with this festival of a completely different section of iTune-era popular music.

A few eager, stunned pop journalists set inside the inappropriate camp preparing for Neil Young and Bruce Springsteen – as far away from Jackson as Kerouac and Pynchon – made a brave, clumsy stab at eulogising Jackson and his achievements. They tried to cleanly separate the groovy, dreamy, gleaming pop music Jackson who bound the rock song with dance beats, the synthesiser with soul, the Jackson that slid swiftly backward while appearing to walk forward, from the sleazy, unearthly and scorned remnant that had been slowly turning to stone for years. Some mentioned Jekyll without Hyde, some mentioned Hyde without Jekyll, some mentioned them both, finding it impossible to talk of the evangelical daylight adventurer without acknowledging the savage night-time demon. If someone concluded that Jackson represented the very best in American popular music, you couldn't help wonder about the other Jackson, the one that publicly enshrined something squalid, peevish and malignant at the heart of America. And then you'd wonder if it was tactful, if it was ultimately a mean disservice to the unblemished pre-grim Michael, at a time like this, in the shimmering, excitable TV minutes following the announcement of his death, to grumpily bring up the dark side of the man, and stumble into the seething mysteries of his ego, and the exhaustion, the mock-biblical grandeur and the exasperating moral zaniness.

Watching others deal with the problem by seeming not to think it was even a problem didn't help me at all to work out whether I had anything to say about Jackson, as opposed to having anything to say about a caricature, a media-assembled monster, a glimpse of a glimpse of someone we only ever really witnessed when he was making some kind of exhibition of himself, gloriously, curiously or repulsively.

It did make me see how the news bulletins were of necessity remembering a very compressed, simplified version, one that could easily be labelled as some kind of tragic legend, that everyone had their own Jackson to remember, and that really the only way to respond to the death in an effusive broadcasting context was to decide which area of his life you might be an expert in, and simply concentrate on that. Find a fragment of Jackson, a shiny, densely actual one or a gruesome, drugged one, something to revere or revile, a small corner of coherence, a chink of light, and stick to examining that.

I agreed to do the radio interview. Perhaps speaking my thoughts aloud on a live show under pressure of particular questioning and the fact that someone else was about to follow me might help me work out what exactly those thoughts were.

It was midnight, about an hour after what during the day had seemed a standard mischievous internet rumour – Michael Jackson had suffered a heart attack, he was dying, he was dead – had turned out to be, once and for all, true. Before I did my phone interview with the radio station looking for a three-minute summary of the passion of Michael Jackson, I heard an expert talk to the BBC about his impressions of Jackson. He remembered watching a suspiciously wrapped up and unexpectedly sturdy Jackson at the O2 launch presentation for his fifty-date residence at the arena. He was struck by how tall Michael was, much taller than the professionally cheery, reliably sensible television host Dermot O'Leary, who introduced him. 'Yes, very tall,' he murmured, as though this was enough of a revelation for anyone to take in at this time of day, faced with such surreally disruptive news. 'Very tall.'

Clearly this particular battle-scarred expert had not been as anxious as me in locating what his approach might be to the news. Or perhaps he really did consider that Jackson's height was significant. Or he was just very tired and emotional. This was in stark contrast to idiosyncratic Jackohistorian Uri Geller, slickly zooming into position with a hustler's pace as leader of the rapidly developing posthumous cult. The hideous and all-knowing spoon-bender was so wide awake I could feel my very soul bend to his glossy will. He clearly was on a mission, as if there was a momentous spiritual vacuum opening up now that Jackson had, no word of a lie, vanished off the face of the earth. Geller obviously had his eye on filling that vacuum himself.

Within minutes of the big gaudy Fox News flash, and the slightly more discreet BBC notice, that Jackson was dead, Geller was revealing that he clearly was some kind of genuine post-Jackson magician by seeming to appear live on three or four news channels simultaneously. He had two pieces of what he told, and indeed sold, as very big news. One, he had once been in a room with Michael – I'm not sure if I lost focus or he did, but each time he told the story, this room seemed to be in a different place, a hotel, his house, Michael's house, cloud cuckoo land – and had asked Michael, as you do, if he was a lonely man. Michael had replied, as you do, 'Uri, yes, I am a very lonely man.' There was a stunned pause from the interviewer, as though this somehow was this incident's equivalent of Jackie O's decision to keep on her blood-splattered clothes while Lyndon B. Johnson was being sworn in as president on the jet carrying JFK's body from deadly Dallas to devastated Washington.

Uri had more to give. He had once, unofficially, hypnotized Michael so that he could ask him a certain question that needed to be answered definitively – had Michael ever interfered sexually with young children? From deep inside one of those deep comas Michael must have had some experience of, Uri, deep inside his own tunnel-vision, got the answer he had presumably been expecting – a simple, sure 'no'. There was another pause, as though this was this incident's equivalent of the news that Diana was in fact pregnant when she died. The look in Uri's eyes as he dropped this news from the great height of his smugness numbed me enough for me to proceed with my radio interview.

I'd decided to develop some theory I had been toying with about the idea of Michael Jackson and a cartoon world that seemed to be the best way of briefly summing him up – and his gleeful love of another boy who seemed stuck at about the age of ten, with strangely coloured skin and a slightly wonky family. Perhaps in Michael's cartoon world Bart Simpson was his friend – how close, and what they might have got up to, we can only speculate – and so it was no wonder that he contacted the *Simpsons* producers, first of all offering to write his pal Bart a number one single (which became 'Do the Bartman', credited to Byron Loren for contractual reasons, which did reach number one in the UK) and secondly to see if he might actually appear on the show. He eventually appeared in a third season 1991 episode entitled 'Stark Raving Dad', well before stars routinely gave their voices to the show as themselves. Jackson, again, ahead of his entertainment time. (The episode was shown again on Fox on 5 July as a tribute to Jackson.)

Michael didn't quite play himself. He was the voice of the large lumbering mental patient, Leon Kompowski, a bricklayer from New Jersey, who suffered from the delusion that he actually was Michael Jackson. Therefore in this cartoon Michael Jackson was 'Michael Jackson' and possibly even further removed from how Jackson looked at the time as the Jackson of the time was from the *Thriller* Jackson.

Jackson apparently was not at all unnerved that he was cast as a crazed twenty-two-stone white man, and his only script requests were that in a joke about mentally fragile pop stars Elvis replace Prince, and the inclusion of a scene where he stays up all night writing a song with Bart. He also asked that an apparent sound-alike (John Jay Smith) be credited with supplying the voice, always a big fan of keeping people guessing.

When Bart's father Homer meets Leon in the New Bedlam mental institution where he has been sent after being mistaken for a free-thinking anarchist, Leon introduces himself by saying, 'Hi, I'm Michael Jackson, from the Jacksons.' Michael is using his soft, sappy, defenceless voice, especially incongruous coming out of the large, shapeless Leon. Homer replies, 'Hi, I'm Homer Simpson, from the Simpsons.'

In the episode, Bart has not brought his sister Lisa a present for her eighth birthday. She's very hurt by this. When Leon and Homer are released from the institution, Bart gets Leon's help to write a special song for Lisa's birthday. Jackson did write the song, the short, very sweet 'Lisa, It's Your Birthday', 'which Lisa says is the best birthday present she has ever had', but he did not sing it, also for contractual reasons. (No doubt paid to speak but certainly not to sing.) The song for Lisa was sung by a plausible and genuine sound-alike, Kipp Lennon.

The forced amusement initially shown by the disc jockey interviewing me on the other end of the line soon drained away when it became clear that all I was going to talk about was Michael Jackson as Leon Kompowski. It disappeared completely when I began to wonder whether 'Lisa, It's Your Birthday' was truly one of Michael's better songs in the '90s, and his guest appearance a little hint of a sign of the awareness Michael had, at least up to the early '90s, of how to play around with people's minds and their perception of his unusual existence.

I wondered on air, rambling a little I admit, how many minutes of Michael Jackson music will truly stand the test of time, compared to, say, the Beatles, or Dylan or Prince, how long it would take in order to play the very best of his songs – I decide just over an hour, and to include 'Lisa, It's Your Birthday', when I am thanked for my time, and that time is in fact over. I have, perhaps, been seen as being just a little too ironic considering it is still, certainly in America, the day that he has died. I have, it seems, misjudged the mood, even though I am very sincere about that thought concerning how many minutes of classic music Michael Jackson actually released, certainly in relation to the amount of very professionally designed secondary music, more than filler, but less than stupendous, that was arranged on his handful of solo albums, not counting greatest hits collections, he made since 1979's *Off the Wall*. It is some sort of compliment that he transformed himself into such a musical legend based on so very few undeniably excellent pieces of commercial art.

Perhaps I should have said, 'It's hard to believe he had such a huge hit, his first solo number one, with a song about a rat from a horror movie.'

Or 'The Jacksons' 1978 album, *Destiny*, can be seen to anticipate Michael's fifth solo album, *Off the Wall*, and it's got its moments, not least "Blame It on the Boogie" – but that album and its Jackson group successor, 1980's *Triumph*, full of the quaint, stringent synths, disco echoes and antiseptically infectious funk of the time, although as glossy, as built on the sweat and anonymous precision of the best session players available, cannot compete with *Off the Wall* and *Thriller*, and the record-breaking solo destinies of Michael, who crowned himself the king of pop but deserved the title nonetheless.'

Or 'He loved to record his vocals with the lights out. Perhaps it was all those years living in the glare of the spotlight that made Michael more comfortable working in the dark.'

TWENTY-THREE

My radio appearance had ended with me not being hailed as someone who in this incident has access to the equivalent of the Zapruder film of the Kennedy assassination but as someone who was spotted lurking a little too close to the Dallas book depository. Before I made any kind of decision about whether I would do anything like that again, and already the requests had come in to appear on early morning TV and radio shows, from those ignorant of the unfortunate Simpsons incident, I re-read an article I had written for the *Observer Music Monthly* a few weeks before he died.

It was written after an appearance on the ruthlessly easygoing live teatime *Richard & Judy* TV show, which required a certain sort of professional control regarding the overwhelming complexity of pinning the liquid Jackson phenomenon in any kind of fixed place. I wanted to see if it could help me get my bearings, and better appreciate that what was expected from me must not contain a grain of suspicion or sarcasm, and no hint of an old-fashioned easily misunderstood rock critic shrug, of the vagrant thought that wasn't this a tremendous amount of fuss to make about a largely discredited pop singer.

TWENTY-FOUR

(Column written for the Observer Music Monthly, *April 2009)*

I don't know about you, but when I was on *Richard & Judy* to talk about Michael Jackson, which I didn't dream but maybe you did, I said that I would be going to see him at least once, maybe once a week, when he plays all those immense sideshows at the O2 Arena between July and February. I was on the show with a godfather of Jackson's children, the former child actor Mark Lester. He played Oliver in one of Jackson's favourite films, Carol Reed's 1968 musical production, and is now a very levelheaded osteopath living in Cheltenham.

I was aware of the strangeness of the moment, a strangeness I quite enjoy, leading as it does to a certain intoxicating lightness of being, and also that, because I was on the *Richard & Judy* show with a friend of Jackson, it was not appropriate to consider the paranormal side of the Michael Jackson phenomenon nor indeed the oozing creepy side. It didn't seem correct either to explain at length my theories on how the pop universe is such an amazing thing it stretches with scintillating elasticity from the polluted wastes, the hell, of where Jackson now lurks to the glittering life enhancing purity, the heaven, of, say, Camera Obscura, and that there should be a kind of abstract rating system that fences off the nefarious nature of such as Jackson and draws attention to the ideal, idealistic pop of Camera Obscura. It didn't seem right to say, you know, if you love pop, whether the Carpenters, Love, Buzzcocks or Girls Aloud, you should listen to the new Camera Obscura single, 'French Navy'. We were there to discuss the disorientating impending resurrection of Jackson without reference to any hell he may or may not be setting up at home, in a castle the size of his ego.

When discussing Michael Jackson in certain controlled and light-hearted showbiz situations it becomes necessary to block out vast troubling areas of the gothic labyrinth of his life, the grimly occult tangles of stress, loneliness, accusation, freakishness, kinkiness, eccentricity, hypocrisy, addictions, abuse, legal disputes, financial shenanigans, dubious deals, weight loss, skin conditions, panic attacks, scandals and sundry deceptions. Even when the sordid sensationalist details of his unnatural personal saga are touched upon, it is still very much as a response to how a celebrity squirms inside a shredded tabloid representation of sleaze, as though the sicker details of Jackson's life, and indeed his literal physical sickness, is somehow not real, merely a kind of unpleasant side effect of the toxic notoriety that comes with such far fetched international success. The full craziness contained in the thought that this creation, this trembling mortified hybrid of fact and fiction, commerce and neurosis, vacancy and allure actually roams the planet is ignored even when the accusatory tabloid horror at his repulsive otherness is at its most vehement. Jackson's brittle alien presence is taken for granted even as it is being mocked or marvelled at.

As I was talking to Richard and Judy I found the way I was internally censoring my thoughts about Jackson so as to suit the circumstances, wearing my own mask in a way, led to a kind of agitated celebration of this spoiled child star as the ultimate science fiction glam rock star – I stopped short of revealing my suspicions that he's a true spider from Mars, an eerie Warholian manifestation of supernatural self-consciousness, infected charisma, fractured originality, brutalised sensitivity, epic self-pity and performance craftiness, a sneaky, fraudulent version of a human being, a vain, unscrupulous interplanetary wanderer trying to make sense of a planet he just happens to be visiting on his way to other worlds. While here he has disguised himself as an extraordinary entertainer, needing unconditional adulation as a form of nourishment, generated a following of pseudo-religious proportions, and made a few sometimes appalling blunders, almost to the extent of giving away that he is not human. While getting carried away with the self-publicising self-glorifying search for adoration that feeds him he has forgotten the location of his space ship. He cannot make his planned getaway and the whole adventure leads to being found out, panic stricken incarceration and an eventual autopsy revealing that when we thought he was a child prodigy he was in fact over two thousand years old.

And then there is his skin, the skin Bowie as the thin white duke fancied but could never achieve without actually dying and coming back to life. When you think about Jackson's skin too closely it causes a kind of vertigo, an anxiety that its spooky journey from dark to light and lighter and somehow thinner will not stop, leading to a kind of transparency where we will end up seeing his insides, his nerves and brain and heart and blood, and clues perhaps as to how it all turned out this way, how the innocent boy with the sweet voice and the promising moves became an obscene living metaphor for the self-harming violence of fame. I mentioned none of this to Richard and Judy, of course, and listened as Mark explained how normal it is to spend time with Michael, who is actually quite normal – despite the scars, the decaying vigour; the burnt deadness in his eyes which are stretched back further and further from the haunting remnants of his nose; the surgical masks; the scarecrow wigs; the smeared lipstick; the baby dangling; the malignant obsessions; the forlorn protestations of innocence and the ultimately defaced essence.

Mark takes the position of those inside the Jackson camp – he's a nice person who had a bad childhood, there's persecuting cruelty and racism implied in the media-organised assault on his reputation and status, he's the most brilliant entertainer of his generation, the vitally vivid if tantalisingly vulnerable singing dancing idol that has influenced the image manipulation song selling media hypnotising actions of every single mass appeal hyper-pop singer since the mid '80s. It starts to sound moderately plausible, give or take that unsettling hole in Jackson's chin, the surreally chiselled jaw line, the tip of the nose that is undoubtedly glued on, and which I heard – allegedly, a key word in this story – once fell off when he was rehearsing a dance routine, to be stood on by a member of his dance troupe who thought he had stood on a snail. And then there's the latest abnormal nose, which rumours have it – rumours, another key word in this story – was built out of part of his ear. The lost bit of his ear was then rebuilt using part of his rib, etc. etc., until all parts of his body have been moved elsewhere to maintain a roughly human shape.

Nevertheless, a sensible Mark proposes that the compassionate, traumatised, unfairly dishonoured Michael is preparing a magnificent return to what he does best, by which I decide he means transform unique internal anxieties and insecurities, a liquid sadness and compacted anger, his fascination with waifs, strays and mutants, into dazzling, highly equipped showmanship. Mark almost officially represented those many who want to maintain the history that Jackson was the extravagant, irresistible latest in line after Garland, Holiday, Presley, Brown and Wonder, and honour the pop-holy version of the young, dream star that ignores how Jackson himself betrayed this version perhaps by assuming that it led to an immunity from punishment for various aesthetic, commercial and moral sins.

A recent MTV poll to establish the greatest album of the past thirty years seems to follow this route and exile all the horror and disfiguring and blight into a vacuum. Forget about what he has done to himself, and allegedly others, just think about the music. Think about the videos. Think about the production of Quincy Jones. *Thriller* was voted number one. In the MTV solar system, of course it would be. Less obviously, Craig David's debut album *Born to Do It* was at number two, which along with the vastness of the pop universe needs some explaining, followed by the more expected, if very white, *Appetite for Destruction*, *OK Computer*, *Nevermind*, *Morning Glory*, U2, Stone Roses, the Arctic Monkeys, Amy, Kanye, Strokes, etc., etc.: the vast pop universe from a fairly fixed local temporal perspective. All led by Jackson. And Craig. I don't think *Thriller* would be in my top 100, and I don't listen to Michael Jackson – although Ian Brown singing 'Billie Jean' and 'Thriller' with elegant wistfulness provides a blissful melancholy echo of the idea of Jackson as soulful, mysteriously motivated hero worth celebrating. I find myself strangely drawn to seeing Jackson at O2 because of his fame, and the way it has eaten into him, and it seems his fans.

Perhaps, because it's my job, allegedly, I would see the first show on 8 July, two or three along the way, and then the final show on 24 February next year, just to see what change there is in his appearance, the show, the audience's relationship with him, the old and new media's treatment of him, what we can tell of what we still call his mind, to what extent the final curtain really is the final curtain, and whether indeed it is still a real Michael Jackson performing or some kind of Jackson-tron, or Thrillerbot. Some say it wasn't actually him at the press launch for his O2 series, and so maybe he will be played by a series of performers each one rep-resenting a certain period in his life, a little like how in Todd Haynes's Bob Dylan film *I'm Not There* it took six actors to begin to scratch the surface of Dylan.

When Michael was the eleven-year-old superstar, the Jackson 5 darling with something sinister lurking in the background as yet largely undiagnosed, the nose on his face was totally his. (This MJ could be played by Keira Knightly and a young Obama child.) It wasn't touched before he became the beautiful smiling and humble thirteen-year-old singing his first number one to Ben the rat. (Will 'Bonnie Prince Billy' Oldham and Taylor Swift as angelic Michael not the rat.) The first adjustment to his nose in the late '70s was apparently a botched job in response to a nose broken during a dance rehearsal. In the crotch-grabbing moon walking glove-flashing '80s, as his fame exploded, his nose imploded. (Usain Bolt, David Blaine, Justin Timberlake, Cate Blanchett, Beyoncé and C3PO to play the imperial Jackson, lead-ing via Susan Boyle, David Copperfield, Peter Andre and Bonnie Tyler to Peter O'Toole, John Barrowman, Mickey Rourke, Katie Price, Cheryl Cole and David Van Day as the ruined and exiled post-nose Jackson.)

Each new release requires new facial surgery, allegedly. Much about him, including his talking voice and wealth, shrivels up. His eyebrows wither. He adopts the harried mannerisms of victimised bully. Any comebacks must come accompanied with appearances on television specials loosely related to celebrity reality shows that are set up to convince those that question his intentions and sexual preferences but which tend to confirm that he is wrecked, corrupt, bewildered, fragile, absent. At best he's an experiment gone horrifically wrong in just how a child star can mature into artistically satisfying adult superstar and then age in public without losing touch with the reality his music and videos once so generously illuminated.

To admit completely that it has all gone beyond Marlon Brando/Howard Hughes/Gary Glitter/Bernie Madoff/Robert Mugabe wrong for Michael Jackson means that our own memories, our own past and the way he fits directly and indirectly into recent history as pioneering superstar presence, have been stained rotten. Perhaps the lingering faith in Jackson as enduring if unstable pop icon as opposed to broken genius with ruptured reputation, a faith that leads to fifty sold-out shows at the O2, is because to admit he is an untamed immature beast means we identified with and supported and ultimately financed something more disgusting and degenerate than delightful. To help Jackson survive the disaster of his downfall and rebuild him as triumphant entertainer is to help us clean up and reorganise history, and absolve us of our own responsibility in allowing such a miserable disintegration to happen.

As Mark finished describing Michael, it seemed quite natural to admit to Richard and Judy that, yes, I would be going to see the Jackson shows. If only for those immense first few seconds, the moment he first appears, surrounded by an enslaved, gyrating Olympic Games Opening cast of thousands and a mighty bass line handed down from above and below, tricking the audience into believing in his telekinetic majesty, washing away all the nastiness, all the rumours and doubts, causing the audience to re-anoint him as their pure and precious King . . . or the first few seconds when his body falls to pieces . . . or the first few seconds as he climbs into the lost space ship he has finally located, and flies back into the stars . . . or when he incredibly begs for forgiveness . . . or when he doesn't turn up.

TWENTY-FIVE

Perhaps I needed to make the role of the mature, clear-sighted and musically open-minded Quincy Jones in the pop construction of Michael Jackson the centre of my response, and examine how it was the very particular history of melting, merging, made over, improvised and composed American music that Jones lightly and proudly carried with him that ultimately created a kind of common-sensical but considerably electric focus for the woozy, self-aggrandising visions of Jackson.

Jones once described being a record producer as being 'part babysitter, part shrink. I'll tell you what it is – it's love. It's loving to work with people you respect. It's a serious love affair – that trust between a producer and a performer. Because sometimes what you're doing is like an emotional X-ray of a human being.'

He built Jackson, the biggest-selling solo performer in pop history, in the studio, with Jackson and for Jackson, creating the sonic fictions we most think of when we think of Michael Jackson, the riffs and horns and feel and rhythms and sudden bursts of grabby action – songs that obviously come out of the Motown and Philly Michael, where Quincy found obvious clues as to why people liked him and his voice, he couldn't miss the charisma and otherness, but Jones treated the idea of Jackson as if he already appreciated that in years to come Jackson would be as massive an entertainment name as anyone he had worked with in music. And that means he treated Michael as someone who would belong in a list that contained Sinatra – his first job for Frank was to arrange 'Fly Me to the Moon', the first music ever played on the moon – Basie, Gillespie, Clark Terry, Tommy Dorsey, Cannonball Adderley, Milt Jackson, Sarah Vaughan, Lionel Hampton and Ray Charles.

Charles was a couple of years older than Quincy, but he was a key figure in Quincy's '40s introduction to a variety of urgent new outsider underground music rapidly coalescing from all points on the compass to form rock and roll, based on how the blues were used to chase away the blues. Quincy was once asked if working with a pop crossover act like Jackson was an unusual move for him, because of his background in jazz. 'Not at all. I've always done that. When I was thirteen years old, during World War II, we were doing that in the nightclubs of Seattle with Ray Charles. We played everything, blues, jump, country, southern soul, strip music, R&B, pop music. Everything! A lot of jazz people came down on me and were talking about how I was stretching out to do Michael Jackson. I said, that's not a stretch. I've been doing it my whole life. I loved Louis Jordan and Debussy, Dizzy Gillespie and Sinatra. I never did one style.'

Quincy grew up amid the type of poverty that means he was driven to frying up cockroaches in order to eat down Seattle back alleys teetering on the edge of civilisation. Jones's clever music-loving but emotionally disturbed mother was institutionalised and his father was a master carpenter. He was musically precocious as a child, neighbourhood vandalising leading to a love for the pure elevating wonder of sound. He would sneak into Seattle dance clubs when he was a small boy. He babysat for a local music teacher so he could read the teacher's books on arranging by Glenn Miller. He was weaned on consummate hybrid entertainers like Cab Calloway, Woody Herman, Skinnay Ennis, became fascinated as a young trumpeter why saxophone sections sounded the way they did, why bass trombones went so low. By 1956, at twenty-three, he was Gillespie's musical director on his state sponsored tours of the Middle East and America.

For Jones, Jackson might be the next stage on from Gaye, Donny Hathaway and Wonder, but he could see how they themselves owed a debt to the explorations and innovations, the wit, ingenuity, humour, spirituality of Miles, Coltrane, Bill Evans and Adderley, to the hip and aware bop and bebop as 'one of the greatest solutions to the racist shit back then'. For Jones hip hop was just bebop flipped through the edited and editing sensibilities of a few driven assimilating rebelling synthesising and technologically manoeuvring generations.

Quincy relished the constantly updated space-age beauties of the recording studio, and if pushed hard to come up with the ultimate reason why the music of Jackson had such appeal and sold so many copies I would say it would be because of the way Jones, like all the truly great record producers, treated the recording studio as the central, guiding instrument of a pop record, much more than the guitar, drums, voice or synthesiser. The recording studio could replicate the adrenaline-driven transformative urgency of someone like Jackson, because the capabilities released by a recording studio were all about the notion of transformation – and of turning feeling and thinking into sound, which to some extent existed in the same place as feeling, outside the body, inside the soul, beyond easy definition.

If we think of the *Off the Wall/Thriller/Bad* Jackson as the equivalent of a kind of sculpture that turned into a fixed but constantly fluid state, a particular vision, in one sense, then Michael Jackson is a gallery looking for a very particular shape and texture. Quincy Jones is commissioned as the artist dreaming up the idea and design based on the specific taste and desire of the gallery, and then in turn using others to help build and execute the finished piece – to make it real. Quincy built this model of Michael Jackson, one that ended up being an intensely accurate symbolic rendition of Jackson's complex relationship with himself and his audience, inside the recording studio. Michael Jackson is a complete studio creation, and perhaps the trouble we have understanding any kind of 'real' Jackson is because the Jackson we think of only existed inside the imaginations of those using the recording studio as an instrument to create a multi-dimensional illusion that would be labelled as 'Michael Jackson' – and which Jackson himself believed in a little too solemnly – but which was not actually a person.

It was a sonic fabrication, a powerfully drawn character, an invented personality created inside the recording studio that took on a life of its own. The Michael Jackson we had to deal with, and indeed he had to deal with, was made up on this incredibly sophisticated instrument, and the fact that it ending up walking the earth was the equivalent of a character leaving a novel and having to exist in an outside world. (In that sense, comparing this recording studio construction of a myth to how the Beatles were conceived inside a recording studio and then entered the real world suggests one area where Michael Jackson did break through his own limits and enter history as a dramatically positive figure.)

Quincy, as the artist being hired by Michael Jackson as the figurehead of a company representing the interests of Michael Jackson to come up with the best possible musical combination of originality and accessibility, is perhaps closer to the Michael Jackson we think we are talking about when we think of the Jackson of this period. Quincy is Jackson because he is making up from scratch the musical Jackson, even if under the instructions, direct or indirectly, of Jackson himself: perhaps, more accurately, the recording studio is Jackson, so perfectly did Jones use it to build a very particular character. Jackson and co. would later obviously commission other musicians, technicians and engineers to fabricate a sonic version of himself, but no other recording studio operator and technical illusionist came close to Quincy in inventing such a convincing Michael Jackson.

It needed a considerable team of technicians and players for Quincy to operate this recording studio instrument, and a mysterious combination of scientific knowledge, immense patience and imaginative flexibility, but all pop music, whatever the instrumental line up, whatever the sonic ambition, whatever the apparent organic essence of the sound, is made on and because of this complicated, intimidating instrument. To be able to control it so that you can create sound that has a completely distinctive sonic signature, so that you can make out the artistic owner of a song even if you are only hearing the drums or bass, requires a set of skills that were at the time, because of accelerating technological advancements, brand new, and which within years were already largely obsolete. For Quincy, the studio was a kind of church, and it produced a kind of prayer.

'I love recording studios. That's why I never had a studio in my home – to me a recording studio is a sacred, hallowed place. I used to have a saying, "Let's always leave some space to let God walk through the room." Because you're looking for very, very spiritual and special moments in a studio. It can't just be some place you hang out and take for granted.'

Jones's experience in the recording studio went back to the days when they were the equivalent of a penny farthing and travelled the couple of decades to an era when they were a form of space shuttle. Both extremes of mobile sophistication were still devoted to the magical idea of capturing sound, which is a series of thoughts about itself, a sequence of pulses and noises that disappear as soon as they appear, and keeping it in a state where it could last forever. The key was to ensure that this risky technological capturing didn't just merely literally copy a sound but somehow factored into that sound an individual atmosphere and a kind of metaphysical soul print that accurately represented the emotional and psychological intention, the psychogeographical and intellectual history, the personal story behind – and in front of – the making up of this sound.

Quincy first worked in a recording studio in 1951 with Lionel Hampton. A member of Hampton's band, he toured with him, at a time when Hampton was bigger than Armstrong and Ellington. He started recording when you recorded in mono straight to 78-rpm disc. The sound had to be mixed absolutely correctly as it was all happening; there was no mixing desk. What you heard was what you got.

Stereo recording changed everything. For Quincy, it was the future, even as the major labels ignored it. Jones became a passionate advocate of stereo, and pushed it hard. He worked on one of the first stereo records, in 1958, *The Genius of Ray Charles*. He produced Lesley Gore's 'It's My Party'. Jones worked in the early days of the vocal overdub, the layering of the human voice, to produce a new kind of harmony, a transcendental, synthetic human choir appropriate for an exciting, tumultuous new era. It would take an hour just to get one overdub sorted out. He'd call up producer pal George Martin during Beatles sessions so that they could congratulate each other for managing 'to have gotten one extra voice on tape!' (Quincy was continually adept at rounding up the best, most connected consultant and allies in pursuit of the best sounding records. In the early 1980s, when I was working in the studio with the record producer Trevor Horn on records for Frankie Goes to Hollywood, Art of Noise and Propaganda, I remember Jones calling Trevor as he worked in the early hours and picking his brains about how he was using the studio, still working to keep up to date with what you could achieve in the studio. He talked about the new sampling machines, various forms of obscure sound-bending machinery, how did Trevor get this sound, that sound, the flamboyant post-punk disco of ABC, the out-of-this-world music of Malcolm McLaren, the dynamic dream-within-a-dream Teutonic precision of Propaganda. I would hear the result of those conversations in his work with Michael Jackson later, especially in the electronic grandeur of *Bad*. Quincy would be having similar conversations with another superlative pop producer of the time, Nile Rogers, who was applying his highly prized avant-dance post-Chic skills at harnessing space and rhythm, melody and fame, sex and noise with David Bowie and Madonna. These artistic, entrepreneurial commercial producers were always on the move, utilising new equipment and cracking new codes in a perpetual drive to make the very best sounding pop records.)

Jackson first worked with Jones on the soundtrack for the 1978 film version that an all-black cast was making of *The Wizard of Oz*. Diana Ross was Dorothy and Jackson was the scarecrow. Rumours naturally suggested he liked his costume so much he would wear it home. Jackson took to Jones and his love for music that seemed to share Jackson's own sense of music as a kind of saviour. He had wanted Quincy to produce one of his early solo albums, an important part of how he could distance himself from his older brothers as he definitively left behind his very odd teens, and his stressful role as compliant miracle kid. His record company wasn't convinced. By the time Jackson reached his fifth solo album in 1979, getting the hits, but nothing world shattering, certainly not artistically, it took management intervention to persuade a dubious record company that Jones, the writer of movie scores for *In Cold Blood*, of music for TV shows like *Ironside*, was the man to usher Jackson to a new pop level. No one anticipated exactly what that level could be, except perhaps Quincy and Michael.

'The record company said Michael couldn't get any bigger,' Jones once said. 'We fixed that.'

The first four solo Michael albums might have sold a few copies here and there, and he wasn't exactly an obscure singer, but they were never going to make history, or suggest that he had much of a future as an indelible artist. *Off the Wall*'s urgently inviting opening track, 'Don't Stop Til You Get Enough', written by Michael, with the demo intro percussion of Michael's sister Janet and brother Randy still intact, immediately thrusts the possibility of a new self-determined self-styled Michael into place, with a composed but explosive, epic but relaxed, busy but spacious sound, perfectly tailored to cleanly set up his urgently demanding vocals. All the disciplined thrills, fills and spills elements of the new Jackson sound were already in place – lush, levitating strings from disco, swanky, swashbuckling horns from big band jazz, deft, crystalline guitar from funk, molten, elemental bass from soul and R&B, worked up Latin-singed cymbal simmering percussion from everywhere, voice from gospel, pop, Motown, Philly, Jackson's own history, all of it held in space and fixed in time by Jones in his recording studio with his carefully assembled team of engineers and session musicians. Michael was part of a new family business, one more to his taste.

Jones calmly recalled that his big band experience helped him organise all the sounds, and whatever else the track was, it was an incredible, inspired act of methodical organisation. Outside the studio, on the radio, in everyday life, it just sounded like a great, uplifting, pop record, almost purely a gesture of defiant spontaneity capturing moments inside moments as they happen, for the sake of getting even with the bad things in life, even though its appearance of one-off exuberance had been carefully pieced together by Jones and company from assembled bits and pieces of technology, history, musicianship, ideas, excitement, conversation and, of course, Michael. (Quincy encouraged Jackson to also sing newly low on these songs, as on 'Rock with You', another break with the Motown system, which favoured the purely high, unclouded dynamite choir boy Michael. The commitment Quincy gave to perfecting the deluxe Michael Jackson studio sound, without which Jackson was just a bopping chart anybody, paralleled Jackson's own professional dedication to working for hours on his dancing, perfecting every kick, gesture, movement so that they came together precisely. Jones factored into the intricate but accessible new Michael Jackson sound a cascading multitude of sonic moments and platforms and deviations that could inspire sudden motion, quick change and frozen reaction that best showed off Jackson's body breaking abilities. He turned Jackson's fluid but jagged movement into sound.)

The Quincy Michael never strayed far away from this detailed studio blend of shine and energy, drama and attack, tension and release, electronics and zest, expert musicianship and studio trickery, disco drama and funk commotion, pop air and jazz grace, whether he was mooching as a melancholy lost little boy through a broken-hearted ballad, or maintaining his monumental relentless self-regarding energy as he shot forward into his truly fantastic future life.

Off the Wall was a solo album – solo Jackson meeting, shadowing, dissolving into solo Jones – but the sound was made by a team of fairly anonymous musicians used to performing isolated studio duties on the instructions of a producer searching to generate and capture unpredictable energy, and by technicians given the task of ensuring all the work put into the song writing and playing was recorded, mixed and balanced in ways that finished off the music with an unparalleled sound that could only belong to those songs and that playing. 'The collective is always more powerful than the individual,' said Jones, who gathered together many of the same musicians and technicians when Quincy and Michael were reunited for the second solo album.

TWENTY-SIX

After Michael Jackson's death, common digital mourning practices emerged on a variety of platforms. Testimonials and goodbyes poured into Michael Jackson's MySpace page. Facebook saw a similar influx of grievers on Jackson's main fan page and in newly created groups. At its peak, the conversation about Michael Jackson's death on Twitter proceeded at a rate of seventy-eight tweets per second. What can be said about this massive body of tweets? What sorts of emotions did people express about Michael Jackson's death?

APPENDIX B

Typology of Tweets with examples

Objective: Reporting sadness as news, part of updates on tweeter's life
It is a sad day

too caught up in wimbledon . . . but still saddened by MJ's passing.

Feeding the baby and feeling sad about Michael Jackson! He left us too soon!

Shocked by Michael Jackson's death. Such a sad, sad day. Going out for a couple of sales calls, late.

Emotion: Simple expression of sadness
I am sadden by MJ's death . . .
RIP Michael

Emotion: Personal sadness/extreme sadness
I'm devastated about Michael Jackson. What a sad day!!!

it sunk in . . .MJ is gone.. as don lemmon put it, 'Michael Jackson's music is the soundtrack to my childhood' . . . my life. i'm sad . . .

Emotion: Rant, expressing frustration at the media
i'm sick and tired of hearing about MJ's death, yes he died, that's sad. Just leave the man alone already!

i get mj's death was tragic but does it have to be shown everywhere?

Commentary/Editorial: Regret
It's so sad that he died so young

Commentary/Editorial: Chastising others for what appeared like forgiveness of his 'sins'; sad used as 'pitiful'
So Michael Jackson died today . . . like i care.. I am more saddened about Farrah Fawcett's death then a shiesty child molesters death . . .

Am I the only not pretending to be sad about Michael Jackson? He was a child fucker . . . remember?

I hope I'm not offending my friends for not being sad over MJ's passing. I won't be sad when OJ dies, either.

Humour: Making light of something about the event
Is watching the rerun of Michael Jackson night on *American Idol*. Suddenly sad in a completely different way ;-)

From 'Detecting Sadness in 140 Characters: Sentiment Analysis and Mourning Michael Jackson on Twitter'

TWENTY-SEVEN

Off the Wall as the personalised select sound of Michael Jackson and as a commercial monolith turning Jackson from everyday pop star into one-of-a-kind superstar would take some beating. The first day that Quincy and his team started recording *Thriller* at the Westlake

Audio's A studio on Beverly Boulevard, he turned to the leading contributors there for the start of recording – including Michael, so the story goes, like Jackson was a player on his team and he was his coach, his favoured and favourite long-time recording engineer Bruce Swedien, the Cleethorpes-born composer Rod Temperton who wrote central Jackson songs such as 'Rock with You' and the title tracks from *Off the Wall* and *Thriller*, drummer Leon Ndugu, percussionist Paulinho Da Costa, Louis Johnson of the Johnson Brothers – and said: 'OK, guys, we're here to save the recording industry.'

'Now that's a pretty big responsibility,' noted Swedien, whom Jones first worked with in 1958, 'but he meant it. That's why those albums and especially *Thriller* sound so incredible. Everybody who was involved gave 150 per cent. Quincy's like a director of a movie and I'm like the director of photography and it's Quincy's job to cast it.'

Thriller is perhaps the album it is, breaking all the records and reaching further than *Off the Wall*, because the elegant, imperturbable Quincy, military minded, in the right place at the right time, working with the right commercial phenomenon, managed to fix the sleek, clearcut session playing with the honed, horny disco-funk with the revolutionary new technology with the contemporary cultural atmosphere, and make everyone involved believe that the work they did on this album, in their area of expertise, given all the creative freedom they needed, whether mix engineer, drummer, guitarist or Michael

Jackson, would be around forever. This is all Quincy's way of saying he's a believer in togetherness. This is Quincy's way of making things with love.

In the end, however you define and explain the commercial and cultural *Thriller* phenomenon, the basic fact is that everything happened because of nine songs that together last just forty-two minutes, even though years of thinking, planning, experience, love, discovery, dream and desperation went into those forty-two minutes. The album was released just before Christmas 1982, at the very end of the vinyl age, almost bringing it to an end, a celebration and a salutation, and was sequenced very carefully by Michael Jackson and his wise, unruffled and perceptive producer. Jones and Jackson were devoted connoisseurs of the two-sided long-playing record, still a relatively youthful art form, but destined, naturally, not to grow old, as though in the end its basic creative lifespan, give or take a lingering, sentimental mourning period, would be about twenty-seven years.

Throughout the measured twenty-minute-a-side *Thriller* there was a constant sense of a build-up of tension and release, of ebb and flow, calm and storm, revelation and discretion, pulse and exhortation, with songs built to open and close one side or another, coming before one song, or after another, existing in their own world, but also in the other worlds that orbited and abutted them. *Thriller* would eventually become known as the album that contained seven hit singles, as if there was something intentionally cynical and commercially exploitative about that fact, and there may well have been, but it began life carefully constructed as an album, a musical artwork, one atmospheric piece, that just happened to be filled with songs so melodic, distinctive and visual, they took on other, very videoed cultural lives separate from the album.

Jones's methodical approach to the recording meant that the sound, for all its consumer-friendly technological gloss, would brilliantly fuse dandy, wised-up black power with spic-and-span, almost neutered white precision. This tendency to use whatever musicians worked, regardless of their colour, background or genre was something Jones began developing in the late 1950s when recording his own big-band albums, *The Birth of a Band* and *The Great Wide World of Quincy Jones*. Quincy constructed a unique musical life out of making something special from a mix of musicians, singers and stylists that followed the rhythm, and went with the flow, rather than worry about appearance and category.

Somehow, throughout *Thriller*, devil-may-care funk, generous swing and ethereal soul were diligently diluted and expertly modified without losing their essential fierce tang in order to reach the conventional sort of fussy, prejudiced and uptight white audience that would make Jackson truly, internationally popular. Jones helped channel decades of rapid, restless black musical progress – ragtime, jazz, blues, swing, gospel, rhythm

and blues, rock and roll, soul, funk, disco, where a marginalised people boldly found their voice, staked their
claims, opened up reality on their terms and demanded
equality – into the timid, spoilt and jittery white mainstream by exploiting the then relatively new world of
electronic music, with its own border crossing, indefin-
able energies and a whole new universe of fresh sonic
possibilities.

Thriller is in many ways – for all its showbiz-changing
operatic excess, its formulaic machine-tooled approach
to swish, show-off dynamics that were clichés in jazz
but deeply refreshing in pop, and now its permanent
dazzling reputation as the biggest-selling non-greatest
hits album of all time, the peak-performing vinyl-age
product of all time, the last of its type in a way – as
much an earnest, jaunty example of studio-processed
and programmed electropop as it is a classy, aspirational
piece of Prince-minded, groove-based African-American
showmanship. Jones was always on the lookout for new
tricks and gags, for modern, impulsive, hopefully funky
ways to extend the range and impact of music.

Thriller is a perfect example of motivated, high-tech
America, but it's also conceptually connected to the
cerebral European art and history of Kraftwerk of avant-
garde Germany and Giorgio Moroder's synthetic Donna
Summer disco-theatre, and even the pop-saturated Eng-
lish eccentricity of Soft Cell, Heaven 17, Yazoo and The
Human League. It is electropop, albeit on a grand scale,

as much as it is rooted in the more obvious history, the more traceable attitude, of Sister Rosetta Tharpe, Little Richard, Otis Redding, Ray Charles, Stevie Wonder, Tina Turner, Smokey Robinson, Gladys Knight and Jackie Wilson. A mesmerising hybrid of vocal soul and apparent mechanical soullessness. (Jackson and his people did once ask Kraftwerk if they would produce him, suspecting that their methods of modelling music, sculpting rhythm and generating cultural noise would suit Michael's futurist mindset. They declined. He would have interfered with their own carefully maintained speculative strangeness, swamped their own image and methods of presentation with something a little too unlikely. Or perhaps not unlikely enough.)

Just in case the bracing mechanical electronic sounds with their wonderfully moving abstract novelty effect combined with the exuberant, still-intact spicy blackness troubled conservative listeners, anxious that there were oblique subversive messages demanding some sort of revolution, Jones ingeniously folded in the whitest, straightest, blandest music of all into the formula – the creamy, ingratiating and aloof West Coast soft rock of Toto. Their music was so accomplished and undemanding, so shielded from the darkening rays of the sun and the enlightening ways of art, so lacking in disruptive personality, it possessed its own kind of slick exoticism, a form of maverick incuriosity that perversely spilled over into dreaminess. *Thriller* is in some form a Toto album featuring very special guest star Michael Jackson, a baroque, corny, middle-of-the-road, grown-up rock-soul album smartly disguised as an awesome, self-conscious Michael Jackson dance-pop extravaganza. One form of weightlessness meets another, and all heaven breaks loose.

Toto were known as the 'session cat's revenge band', the defiantly unstylish house band of the corporate America music industry, an uncharismatic team of ace, faceless Los Angeles studio musicians guaranteed to satisfy a world-class perfectionist producer's demanding musical needs in the last days before computer manipulation could generate necessary fidelity and tightness and replicate exactness, even transcendence. They had played with invisible impeccability on records for such as Jackson Browne, Eric Clapton, David Crosby, Sheena Easton, Earth, Wind and Fire, Rickie Lee Jones, the Jefferson Airplane, Rod Stewart, Loggins and Messina, Spinal Tap, Paul McCartney and on Quincy Jones's own records, as robotic and manageable as musicians could be before the robots took over, with just enough presence of something disobedient and possibly rebellious. Just enough hint of what some still called rock'n'roll, and some still do.

They formed their own group in 1976 to make a name for themselves, and a ton more money for their highly professional, clean-cut sins. Toto guitarist Steve Lukather, with keyboardists David Paich and drummer

Jeff Porcaro, were main members of the house band Quincy used for the solo Michael records, a central part of his custom-built studio pop orchestra. It's the mellow, literal, easy-listening adult rock of Toto that Jones used to smuggle the sparkling post-Motown, the ardent funk, the electronically framed, far-fetched Jackson into the resistant, wider, familiar rock world, which despite and of course because of the recent status quo-dismantling outbursts of punk and disco was becoming increasingly settled in its ways.

Thriller started with a bang, well, with three urgent percussive rim shots, with an entertainment advocate's promiscuous warning. It started with a classic, deeply confident song about starting something, for real. Beginning the album with such an announcement, with such a perfect blend of imagination and knowledge, immediately makes clear Jackson and Jones mean business, dynamically displaying their belief that this is how a great album should open, with a call to arms, a pop culture call to prayer, tumbling with targeted, rapt, irresistible emotion – a calibrated criss-crossing two-chord frenzy of quips, riffs, rhythms, effects, rhymes, slogans, twists, borrowing freely from funk history, African pop, spiritual intensity, demonstrative soul immediacy, written for *Off the Wall* but now existing as a link between that and the more sophisticated, let's face it more monstrous *Thriller*.

'Wanna Be Startin' Somethin'' was a taut launch pad

sampling all of Jackson's intermingled musical interests: the rampant macho hard rock and the unbridled disco, the deep soul and the glossy pop, the sudden, absurd bursting-into-song American show tunes and the intro-verted, vulnerable ultra-tender ballads, previewing much of what was about to happen on the rest of the record, taking up six minutes, and two important seconds, before the charge deliberately, almost provocatively sub-sides into the solidly, politely mid-tempo, fastidiously palate-cleansing 'Baby Be Mine'. Here's a coy glance at Prince, creating his own crazy world elsewhere, a way of Jackson saying, yes, I can see and hear what you're doing, all that vamping and revamping, but I've got my own plans, somewhere between being more sentimental than you can ever be, but also more heated, and there-fore more extreme. My life – and death – beats your life and death. My pop stardom will outwit yours.

One of the two songs from the album that were never single releases, the near-generic imitative compe-tence makes the previous track now seem even more of a ravishing blast of gutsy confrontational joy, a feeling exaggerated even more because 'Baby Be Mine' then becomes 'The Girl Is Mine', the chaste, floaty, on-top-of-the-sheets, Toto-contained soft-rock duet with Paul McCartney – each of them doting on each other, like brothers, like highly self-regarding but confused living legends, like strangers who could never escape a momentous strangeness, however much they draped themselves in the happy endings, cheers and sympathy of neurotically gorgeous, audience-consoling melodies. The invited listener is dropped into a woozy, almost trippy limbo, a long way from the ominous, combative sound of the opening piece. A nice, sterilised world is carefully pieced together, one that everyone can visit without fear of being scared off by otherness, ugliness or shifty dark shadows.

You're drawn into a gauzy sentimentality that reflects Jackson's anxious, broken desire for comfort and stability, for a safe place, music that's still otherworldly but stripped of rakish menace. Sometimes Jackson uses music to find himself, to work himself out, and celebrate the discovery, and sometimes he uses music to lose himself, to forget all his problems, to go into hiding, as if he's just an ordinary man, a stable, winsome insider entertainer with a clear conscience and a fair amount of self-control, not some trapped, perverse, chronically wary outsider whose crazed impulses and appetites, and lack of human specificity, verge on the freakish and ultimately the threatening.

But then performer Jackson and bandleader Jones as foxy sonic illusionists are lulling us into a false sense of security, temporarily pretending that the evolving Jackson isn't that far removed from the merely attractive, gifted teen, pre-Quincy Jackson of the 1970s, the industry-packaged black Donny Osmond, before they abruptly renew their bright assault on the history of pop with perfectly placed vigour. Across four songs that sensationally capture his glamorous mental agitation and disruptive body blurring, shape-shifting physical grace, and a fair amount of his pile-driving arrogance and sweetheart naivety, Jackson the child star, the recently liberated performer, is given unprecedented creature energy and thrust into the new decade, boosted into a tumultuous, collapsing future. Along the way, Jones and Jackson just happen, as if it was in their original notes, to rearrange the history of pop.

The album ends what was then known as Side One by taking off into the first of these four songs, 'Thriller' itself, pop as a boisterous theme park ride, with potent hack composer Rod Temperton's business-like melodramatic hybrid of shining disco splendour and cornball horror driven by Jones's unleashed post-swing synths – Count Basie chewing up Kraftwerk – all seeming too loaded with picturesque action and tension to merely be the last track on Side One of an everyday commercially released album.

The title track gives us some radiant clues about how Michael Jackson actually perceived the world – about his hopes, fears and aching desire for something he couldn't quite resolve, about the special other dimension he could reach and somehow share when he sang, about how raw, raging performance helped him emerge out of the dark and into the light, and Quincy and co. captured with brimming, delirious sureness Jackson's fierce impertinence, disordered confidence and perversely nerveless, often scandalous determination. A determination to be himself, to own himself, which was enough to drive him mad, as if he realised in his early teens how hard the self is to find, how many others own you, and which here builds up to such a crescendo, it needs some sort of interval, a break in time, a moment where nothing much happens, which once upon a time was the end of Side One and the turning over of things. Temporarily, a blankness beyond the self and beyond the object.

In the days of the album and its unavoidable, very special separate sides, you were always taking off, and landing, in some fixed order or another. The taking off and landing, the moving between different states, between different routes to the same thing, the different ways of experiencing and playing with time, meant the album's format, its basic shape, the length of tracks and the time-fracturing spaces between them, influenced the very nature of song writing. There was for a while the constant construction of whole new worlds, a process and series that could never be maintained, only revived and reworked, once the two sides became one, and lost their shape, and then became pretty much nothing at all, totally shapeless.

Where *Thriller* ended up as a Long Player, as theatre split down the middle, the world of Side Two, on the other side of the looking glass, begins with 'Beat It', which manages the apparently impossible task of both following up the volatile crowd-pleasing adventure of 'Thriller' – which on compact disc it immediately follows – and being even more of an insubordinate mission statement than 'Wanna Be Startin' Somethin''. Written by Jackson after he was goaded by Jones to come up with something as urgent, universal and to the youth-defining p-p-power pop point as 'My Sharona' by The Knack, pop music as inane glory, he sings it like he's got an awful lot on his mind, and a few puzzling, raunchy things to confess, but he's found a way to get out from under all the mounting pressure and dance all the way to the moon, and not stop there.

'Beat It' is famous for the point-blank, genre-shredding guitar solo given as a gift by rock-solid hard-rock guitar hero Eddie Van Halen. ('I did it as a favour for Michael. My band and management thought I was mad. Maybe Michael will give me dance lessons some day in return.') The free solo achieved lift off in a largely unmapped and unzipped zone where zesty, choreographed black pop encountered revved-up white noise. Lukather played all the other guitars on 'Beat It', instructed to find an urbane, even blasé way to bind Van Halen's wild, on-the-fly solo and some haphazard percussion. He was quite capable of quickly and solemnly calculating the necessary details and contriving the only solution possible. Toto remain the slick, no-nonsense backing band even on the furious, neo-nonsensical rush of 'Beat It', which is a little like learning that Crosby, Stills and Nash once backed James Brown. Van Halen himself referred to

Toto as 'collectively, the best musicians on the planet', and it was this level of straight, rock-approved ingratiating and dispassionate expertise that Jones exploited as part of the opulent Jackson template.

Following 'Thriller', 'Beat It' and 'Billie Jean', the fourth track in this astonishing middle sequence, the third track on Side Two, will in fact be a feathery-smooth, Toto-ish song, 'Human Nature', written by Toto's Porcaro with skilled lovey-dovey lyricist John Bettis – who wrote the glistening words for The Carpenters' 'Goodbye to Love' and 'Top of the World' – and this is where the sheer attack of the previous songs dissolves, back into sweeter, easier, pretty much easy-listening life. The fake, expensively conceived old-fashioned show business calm after the futuristic mutant challenges to body and mind that are not so much the result of all the money spent on the recording but of the imagination, which is beyond cost, and time, and to some extent meaning.

The point had been made, Michael's grown up, with surprising new features, he's so tough and sure of himself he can sometimes admit to soppy tendencies, which will earn him a lot of love. 'Human Nature' still makes sense inside the blasted touch-and-go context of Jackson's life, where he needs to break free of a darkening prison, and find sanctuary in rhythm or melody, and Jones electro-propels the song's pillowy self-possession so that this cultured mix of urban black swagger and urbane white decoration becomes an unlikely influence on coming black styles including hip hop crooning and new jack swing.

Before 'Human Nature', in another faraway time, even as it seems close, the contorted grief of 'Billie Jean', written by Jackson, about what might or might not be a real-life situation, and something terribly pertinent he had plaguing his delicate, indignant mind. Jackson 'writing a song' might mean he turned up whilst Quincy's virtuous studio collective got on with building the tracks. He hummed a lyric, clinging to a scrap of melody, chucking in some la-la-la's, hung around for a bit, and left, back to his wonderland, but he's credited with both 'Billie Jean' and 'Beat It', the two undisputed stand-out tracks in terms of their fiery combination of originality and familiarity, as well as the deliberately forceful opening track 'Wanna Be Startin' Somethin''.

Maybe he claimed these tracks totally because they were clearly the stand-out, cliché-crushing tracks, because even 'Thriller' is a little kitschy around the dynamic, ceremonial edges, coming alive through sheer force of Quincy-will rather than evocatively erupting out of Jackson's disintegrating states of mind. Maybe they are the stand-out tracks because Quincy was given the most information about what was required, a better brief, even if this was just some half-formed, nervy anecdotes Michael told about a couple of unlikely recent experiences.

Maybe Jackson had it in him, perhaps in some ways all he had in him, in terms of actual compositional genius – three dead-on classics, seriously motivated by knowing few believed he was capable of delivering such surreal accessibility and musical audacity. Rumours have it that in order to get Michael to sing 'Billie Jean' the way he wanted him to sing it, hard, clear, aroused – without the annoying whoops, coos, squeaks and gulps the often over-worked-up Michael was convinced made him sound strong and in touch with some sort of street-smart ideal – Quincy laid into a wretched Michael curled up on the studio floor. Don't turn this to mush! Michael did it Quincy's way, like he was singing about the real world, as if he meant it, where he was in trouble, hunted, on a knife-edge, and there might be no way out, he might end up incriminating himself. He's seeing red.

Swedien recorded the song as though it was an absolute work of art, full of life and twice as spare, layering the triple synths like air, getting as tight and powerful a drum sound as he could come up with, using the glassy-clean spanking skanky guitar solo David Williams (the B. B. King of the rhythm guitar) recorded for the demo all the way to the finished product. Whenever David replayed the solo, searching for something greater, it was never the same; the moment had passed. It was such unpredictable free-style elements that gave the album, for all the controlled, industrial attention to form and detail, little assertive chinks of spontaneity that keep the sound breathing even as it is set in mighty and eventually mythical stone.

Swedien was left to mix it, more or less on his own – take all those effervescent moments of music and performance living inside their own separate channels, their own isolated world, and bring it all together, as though somehow it was all done at the same time, with everyone in the same room, and mood, and not during a multitude of warped timelines, everyone separated, minding their own business.

Swedien's got some work to do, analysing, grading and grinding down all those fragments of effort and effect and stray, almost lost bits of time and making up a coherent story that flows relentlessly in the direction it has to without any sense of all the edits, merging, retiming, refocussing, chaos, mishaps and layering that goes on. One completely logical and linear performance out of a disjointed scattershot of contributions and collaborations. He listens to all of these moments time and time again, and falls in love with what it could be, the song it will become, with an innocent, music-loving commitment, an integrity beyond corruption. It takes such sober, grown-up attention to detail to produce such distinctive, near-deranged sassiness.

He got lost inside the task and pulled a popular art masterpiece out from inside all his concentration, and the concentration of his collaborators. It's one of the reasons Quincy liked him working for him, was always happy to have him around. Unfussy, undemanding Bruce would get on with making sense of everything, and Quincy could get on with other things, including making more problems for Swedien to solve.

On behalf of Quincy's exceptional studio team, on behalf of Jackson's great, irrational urges, Swedien vigilantly constructs a frisky, chic sonic personality, which is always more than it seems, all those sharp, flashing things, inside a special level of exclusion, with a cooling, illuminated groove, so that even if you just hear a few drum beats of the track, getting going, or coming to an end, you know instantly what the track is. When the firm, festive bass starts up, embedded inside such blessed commotion, all that fanatical control, you get this warm, good feeling that everything will come out all right, and such a feeling can somehow separate you from annihilation. So you're hearing Michael's thoughts in the music, as well as in his voice, and the way the voice and music become one thing, as if this performance was always meant to exist, and just needed finding, deep in the chaos of Michael's life, and life itself. You cannot get further from death than experiencing this expression of the rush and delirium of life, and living, whatever the cost; the basic purpose of pop, perhaps, of great entertainment, the blissful temporary evasion of extinction, the obstinate rejection of oblivion. Something worth singing about, whatever you seem to be singing about.

It didn't come quick, or as quick as it could have done,

this rigorous and prestigious articulation of the art and science of pop music's late twentieth-century power. That's another thing that has to be hidden in the final product; all the decisions that got made, all the indecisions, on the way to finding out what exactly the song was going to sound like, once it was cut, mastered, ready for play, for the shops, for the future, for Michael on stage and screen to make real and more importantly unreal.

After a day or two Bruce had mix number two of 'Billie Jean', which he thought was 'a killer'. Michael, Quincy and Rod Temperton came into the control room to listen. There was a lot of love for it and happy, relieved dancing. The song had become something, because without the right mix no pop song will work and stretch time and space into its unexpectedly correct new shape. Then Michael motioned for Bruce to follow him out of the control room and whispered to him that it was perfect, but it needed a bit more bass, just one more mix. After that was done, Quincy had a thought. He asked Bruce to 'add a little garlic salt to the snare and the kick. Just a squirt!'

Swedien was soon up to mix twenty. And beyond. Half-inch tapes containing versions some might consider almost identical were soon stacked to the ceiling. A week later, mix ninety-one. Perfection! He played it to Quincy, who seemed happy, but there seemed to be a 'but' hanging in the air. He asked, just for the fun of it, to listen to one of those earlier mixes. How about mix number two? What the ...!? Everyone in the control room agreed that this was the one, as though all those other mixes had never even existed, but it would not have been so clear that mix two was the one without those other mixes proving that, even though there were all those possibilities, in the end there was only one true positive way of getting it done.

'Well, here's the deal,' reported Bruce. 'When *Thriller* was released to the whole world by Epic Records on Tuesday, November 30, 1982, it went to Tower Records with mix two of "Billie Jean" on it. And when the single of "Billie Jean" came out it was mix two!'

The success of *Thriller* as an utterly persuasive musical product and as a piece of supreme commercial entertainment was perhaps down to the fact that Quincy, in control of all the things he needed to be in control of, watching over and watched over by Michael, in control in his own way of all the things he needed to be in control of, made more of the right decisions about sound and content than usual amongst all of the thousands of decisions that need to be made when you work on such a complicated enterprise and search for unfamiliar form and meaning that doesn't alienate the masses.

'Thriller', 'Beat It' and 'Billie Jean', because of the big-deal videos that were rapidly becoming so much a part of the pop music effect, completing the overall illusion, and the histories and myths they've ended up being part of, now seem far too big, rich and cinematic, too much their own galaxies, to have ever been simply part of a vinyl album, routinely lifted off to be 7-inch singles after a series of oily corporate meetings around big glass desks in anonymous offices in functional, glowing skyscrapers.

Around them, there are the songs that set them in motion, and eased the pressure, and the songs that take us back from the brink towards reality, so that at the end of Side Two there's the more conventional, but still nifty, 'P.Y.T.', followed by Temperton's slight but astute whimsy, the second non-single, 'The Lady in My Life'. We are gently placed back into the ordinary world we left behind, the one we knew before 'Thriller', which has now completely changed. Nothing was the same after 'Thriller', even if only because Michael Jackson would now be in any number of ways some sort of Monster, as famous, and as famously odd, as anyone else on the entire planet who had ever lived or ever would. At the same time, he comes more real, and not real at all, flying, and frozen, in a place that combines fame with death, and entertainment with immortality.

Somehow, its very inconsistency as a complete album highlighted its amassed power as simply the place where Michael's greatest songs first appeared, one after the other, one ending the first side, and another starting Side Two. Even the tracks that weren't the newly franchised post-disco soul-rock of 'Wanna Be Startin' Somethin'', 'Thriller', 'Beat It' and 'Billie Jean', even including the manly moisture of the Paul McCartney duet and the (naturally, knowingly, naughtily) boy-Prince 'Baby Be Mine', seemed perfectly positioned to showcase, to isolate, to intensify the effect of the tracks that we can now not think of in any other way, as if they have been around forever, and will be around forever.

Whatever you think of Michael Jackson – whether he is, as he wanted, the imperial, adored King of Pop, worthy of a seat at the heavenly high table of show business legends alongside Chaplin, Monroe, Dean, Presley, Sinatra, Lennon, Garland; a radical, intrepid pop artist who bravely and ultimately dangerously challenged social, sexual and racial rigidity; or a ruined, sleazy, bizarre super-celebrity with such paranoid, self-destructive and ungovernable impulses they led to a terrible, trashy early death – *Thriller* is a mesmerising slab of hardcore musical drama that fights to make sense of being alive.

It exists as the built-up climax to a couple of decades of extraordinary energy released by Ike, Elvis and Little Richard, Rosetta, Tina and Aretha, amplified and redirected by the Beatles and Hendrix, by Janis and Jagger, by the soul of Motown, Stax and Philadelphia, by the fractious, reality-grabbing, society-shifting funk of Sly and Parliament, by the glory-hunting outsider white-boy appropriations of Todd Rundgren, John Fogerty and David Bowie, by sex-boy glam and sex-change disco, by the tart, joyous 7-inch pop sensibility of synth-primed new wave, all of which had made it into the feverish, susceptible mind of Jackson. Once his insatiable imagination was jammed into *Thriller*, into this mysterious, tenacious place invented by conscientious humans and bloodless machines, once it became clear that there was single after single available to promote and re-promote the album until millions owned it and the world sang it, Michael Jackson took over in what turned out to be his favourite stage, his favourite show business home – the video, where cinema went pop!, where he could be himself, a space invader of self-invention, half cartoon half human, sinless, stirring image, exemplary energy seen to be in motion as much as heard.

By the time he appeared in the video for 'Thriller', he was already looking a lot different from how he looked on the cover of the album, and that was before the mutant make-up took things to extremes. Transformed into a choreographed zombie, this predicted what was to happen to him in real life, as common human characteristics were systematically burnt away, by personal problems, by vaulting vanity, and the gradual withdrawal of composed, guiding father-figures and transcendent historians like Jones, as weird as the world in his own way. Jackson was more and more alone in a sinister world infested with slack, slippery celebrities, one increasingly fuelled by gossip, disgrace and cruelty.

From now on, Jackson's life would be less and less about the music, despite whatever Jones-induced and post-Jones highs happened on the still sure-footed next album, *Bad*, and the irregular, less progressive ones beyond that, and more and more about his body, and his face, and his obsessions, and the ways skin, sanity, soul and reputation fell apart. *Thriller*, this album about the transformation of music, fame, physical space and black entertainment history, featuring fantasy cameo appearances that only Jackson could arrange, changed Michael Jackson's world to such an extent, he just couldn't stop changing, until he changed so much, he was no more. That he left behind this album and these songs, which live on like frisky, untouchable ghosts, gaining in eerie, nostalgic power as the twentieth century and the music-accelerating world of the album slips away, can make you believe in the supernatural.

TWENTY-EIGHT

Posted by Father Maxxitone on 25 August 2009

'As a priest, musical fanatic and follower of Christ I can only pray that Michael's soul has been received by the Lord Jesus Christ. I had broke down into tears and prayer when news of Michael's sudden death had approached. I believe Michael is indeed in heaven, and I cannot believe in anything else until I reach the heavenly gates myself. As a student of music, I myself have been captivated by Michael's angelic vocals, sweeping dance moves and graceful songwriting. Studying him as a man, as a humanitarian, as a father . . . a man of such

humility and love . . . I cannot picture him in the ghastly pit of eternal suffering. I pray for his children, family, and friends who have been affected by his passing. I also pray for his fans who seemed to have taken it hard. Our God is a god of mercy, love, care, and fairness, and we must remember he sent all of us here on a mission. He sent Michael here to Entertain, bring joy, and show his kind heart to people.

May he rest in eternal paradise.'

TWENTY-NINE

The day after Michael Jackson died, I was asked by the BBC 2 arts review programme *Newsnight Review* if I would go on to the show that evening to talk about Michael Jackson. To Clare, the producer making the call in all innocence, because surely this was my job, as rock critic and regular *Newsnight* panellist, I must have sounded infused with such wearisome self-pity I might actually be related to Jackson himself.

The truth was I had decided overnight, not least because of the *Simpsons* debacle, that I was not going to agree to any requests to comment in the media on the life and death of Michael Jackson. It wasn't like anyone would really miss me – losing out on some vital piece of the analysing puzzle without which none of the collected punditry building up by the minute would make sense. And the thought of it was causing me an indistinct sort of grief, although maybe I was transferring the feelings

I more naturally if subconsciously felt over the death of Jackson over into my professional life.

I explained to Clare that I didn't think I would be much use on the programme, as my thinking about Jackson had become so knotted, and cracked, and a little fishy, as though somehow my response to the death bore as much relation to a really concise and hopefully insightful *Newsnight Review* contribution as Jackson's latest nose did to a normal nose. I had come to the conclusion that in fact Jackson had died at some point between 1992 and 1994, but that due to some uncanny elemental force, the death had not quite 'taken' – Jackson had not been completely removed from life or the planet, and began a strange twilight period where he still haunted the planet, half dead, barely alive, and the rest of us were forced to postpone the grief that was natural to give back then, when it seemed the right time for him to die. We had all been compelled to live through a fifteen-year period where we could not put the whole thing where it really needed to be – actually, in a grave, his grave, so that we could deal with Jackson as it should have been for all these years, as a dead superstar. The raw, giddy response to his death, all the candles, coverage and tweeting, I told Clare about fifteen hours after it had happened, was a massive outpouring of relief that finally we could all grieve and mourn. Reality had somehow realigned itself to where it should have been all along. He was dead, but then he'd been dead before.

I said that consequently my thinking was too twisted up around itself for me to be able to do any light dancing through the musical progression. I'd lost track of whether I was responding to something that had any merit and logic in itself, responding to his music and its essential qualities, as if the story really was as it seemed to be, as if it actually was a case of a creative trailing away after *Off the Wall* and *Thriller*, as *Bad* turned to *Dangerous* turned to *Invincible*, as meaty, integral bits of Jackson's soul and body were left behind every time he pulled off the completion of a Jacksonically conclusive, internationally successful, career-boosting or sustaining or rescuing pop track, whether it was 'Black or White', or 'Scream', or 'Smooth Criminal' – and that I was in danger of dwelling for hours at a time on the meaning of those self-mythologising one-word album titles, and losing my track, and deciding in the end that he was just some grotesquely self-important post-modern day P. T. Barnum who had decided a) attention is good, b) controversy is better, and c) outrage is a gift that keeps giving, and all those attractive and/or not-so-attractive pop songs were nothing more than well- or not-so-well-designed pop songs that were part of the greater plan to simply keep drawing attention to himself, that his music was just him pouring his emotions over his body and then passing it on as if everyone else should care, that the drugs first liberated him and then ruined him, that the more knowing he got the more glassy eyed and screwed up he became, that he and he alone had knocked the stuffing out of the idea that rock and pop had any spirituality or sense of mission, or he was in the end merely a spectacular, sophisticated and sometimes quite raucous collective hallucination calculated to survive for about fifty years and then splutter to an end before releasing a series of oozing flashbacks, tattered souvenirs and fleeting impressions of his role in the late-twentieth-century entertainment age that would last to the end of time.

And then there was a new theory I'd had about Michael Jackson's lyrics, whether they were written by him or commissioned from others to fall in with the raging, tender, paranoid, moonstruck, aphrodisiacal, wistful, victimised, passive house style, the defiance and toughness that acted as a protective armour, the way they seemed to autobiographically feed off his private life, his secret psychology, his deepest feelings, confronting the rumours about his sexuality, the media reports of his dysfunctional habits, the mocking of his taste and whimsies, the way they seemed to tantalisingly confirm that as cruel and contemptuous as the media could be about Jackson's physical and emotional deformities, they were on to something.

I had concluded that in fact these lyrics were themselves written or selected by him in reaction to his increasingly fixed image as malfunctioning celebrity and sexually anxious paranoiac. They were not about any real Michael, they were opaque, behind-the-scenes Michael making up this tragic, defiant public image of Michael as projected on to him by those that were either adoring or condemning the shtick. The words he sang were just another part of his deviant gamesmanship and another method of actually hiding far away who and what he really was: he hid behind the pretence that his songs were faithfully and generously about his feelings, grievances and tribulations. This was what he wanted us to think. There were no clues at all in any of the songs about his secluded behind the scenes true nature except of course that none of them were actually really about him. Only about a fictional portrayal of him. This was how clever and sly a psychedelic huckster he really was. I had no clear follow-up theory about why the hell he would bother being so oblique, other than that he was very cold.

So I was going to find it hard to fondly recall the time he moonwalked on that MTV show and blew the world's mind, as if that was what really happened. I couldn't see Michael Jackson for all the Michael Jacksons that the news of his death had discharged. All I could see was how an over-dressed and over-done, tacky and misshapen Michael Jackson existed because of the way an image had been constructed by various forces and the tensions that continually existed between him and the media and the music business – which he both needed and profoundly distrusted.

Perhaps thinking about all of that released Jacksonia vapour that had occurred once he had died had sent me into a near trance-like state, one that put me very close to actually understanding the vast, tiny mind of Jackson himself, all the clutter, and emptiness, elation and dullness, anger and absence, all that Him, and not-Him, all that Tom and Jerry, E.T. and Wendy, Audrey Hepburn and Vincent Price, White Rabbit and Snow White, ghosts and corpses, swans and treasure, space ships and daydreams jealous fairies and treacherous pirates, sex and waste, fear and drugs that resided there, all those memories torn from their moorings, his inability to fix himself to reality, the way he would float clear of the concrete, the multiplication of doubts, the unthinkable thoughts, the horror of the flesh, the suicide he felt only as an idea never an action, he wasn't lucid enough to go there, the time hanging limp in the still air . . . it was as though I could understand how Michael lived without any limits to his mind and imagination, nothing that could ground him in the necessary everyday. Nothing bound his experiences to his memories and emotions in ways that could give him serious clues about how to function and behave as a reasonably sane human being.

Oddly enough, I still got booked for the show. Perhaps Clare thought that after ranting at her for some minutes I had got it all out of my system, and on the night I would crisply slip into a tidy 'phenomenally ebullient child star betters himself like none before, only to dissolve into the apogee of weirdness' conclusion.

The broadcast went relatively smoothly, although I must admit I was a little disconcerted when one of my fellow panellists commented that what was interesting when it came to Michael Jackson was that in fact there were 'two Michael Jacksons'.

Two? Two! What had I missed? For a television moment I almost sank back into the unravelled spiralling mind of Michael Jackson, all that susceptibility and paralysis, all that frantic menace and insecurity. I caught myself just in time, and interjected that even as recently as the *Invincible* album in 2001, he wasn't that far off being up to his old tricks, give or take the fact that there was nothing left of the body of the Jackson 5 boy. Still, we all grow up, and our appearance changes, one way or another. (You put a photo of me now next to a photo of me at ten and you would conclude that in sad, unfathomable ways I looked nothing like I once did. I too have a very different nose and my hair is in a very different place.)

Meanwhile, even though I had decided I had absolutely nothing to say about Michael Jackson, and I was damned well not going to say it, I had agreed to write a comment piece about the life and death of Michael Jackson for the *Observer*. I arrived back home after the *Newsnight Review* appearance and had ten hours to come up with something, reeling as I was from the 'two Jacksons' comment, an observation that was either true, grounded and revealing in its elementary simplicity, or completely missing the point that Michael Jackson was legion. He was many. And now he was dead he was on his way to becoming many more.

THIRTY

(Comment piece written for the Observer *dated 28 June 2009)*

As soon as he was gone, he was everywhere, regaining a flashy, bewitching agility he hadn't had since the early 1980s when he really was a kind of king. He was everywhere, and everyone had something to say, even if they didn't really know what to say. As soon as it was clear that he was really dead, and that it was now Michael Jackson 1958–2009, the instantly surreal truth of course being obtained and announced not by a traditional media outlet but by a furtive, deadpan celebrity website, a whole host of Michael Jacksons were released into the air. The loved Jackson, the gloved Jackson, the wealthy Jackson, the bankrupt Jackson, the Motown Jackson, the moonwalking Jackson, the MTV Jackson, the despised Jackson, the genius, the mutant, the addict, the oddball, the victim, the black, the white, the creepy, the glorious, the pathetic, the gentle, the monster.

You could take your pick which Jackson you want to remember, which version of the monster, or the genius, or the dissolving man behind the mask. He was everywhere, but now that death had returned his full powers as a spinning, gliding master of self-publicity, any truth about who he really was and what he'd been up to was shattered into a thousand glittering pieces. Once we stayed up late to watch the premier of the 'Thriller' video. Now we stayed up late to watch another form of extraordinary choreography intended to turn one fascinating, paranoid, fiendishly otherworldly entertainer into an immortal.

The crazed rush was on to try and fix just one Jackson in place; the trailblazing star, or the abused innocent, the loneliest man alive, or the greatest entertainer of all time. The uneasy combination of frantic web action and obsessive, hasty, flamboyantly superficial news coverage meant it was possible actually to witness a certain sort of immortality start to take form. The tweeters, the websites, the pundits, the acquaintances, the impersonators, the colleagues, the hangers on, the fan club members, the news readers, the correspondents, the international celebrities all performed their duties so obediently that the whole event seemed to follow a script with the full approval of Jackson. (Imagine how well he'd planned the funeral.)

It was immediately clear that the nature and timing of this end had been coming for such a long time. Even while the whole thing was deeply disconcerting and in the middle of it all someone had actually died, it was also the most obvious thing in the world. Now that it had arrived, this punch line to all the scintillating music and living, seedy chaos, everyone knew their place, as if Jackson's final mortal act as extremely self-obsessed entertainment illusionist was to ensure that the news of his death was itself a kind of glittering if slightly tawdry spectacle.

In those first remarkable moments, death had allowed the myth of Jackson to surge into life, and his career got the focused injection of publicity he had recently been unable to consistently generate without sacrifice. The twenty-four-hour news channels couldn't believe their luck, all this archive, tension, scandal, revelation and gossip. All this Uri Geller. Jackson played a massive, needy part in shaping an entertainment universe which now largely consists of constant gossip about the antics and eccentricities of damaged celebrities, and his death was confirmation that the presentation of round-the-clock news, certainly when it comes to popular culture, is little more than formally presented, gravely delivered, hastily assembled tittle-tattle.

Everything had been destined to lead to this untimely, shady death, and once that death arrived, a certain kind of order was established. Jackson was where he'd been heading all along – a sudden tragic end, a twist of mystery, a sad final trip low across the LA sky to the coroner, coverage that seemed in part pre-recorded ready for the big day. The whole thing concluded the only way it could – in a resounding blast of grotesque but compelling publicity for a figure who had become all that he had become, the king and the imprisoned, the adored and the humiliated, the accused and the indulged, because of publicity. Jackson had been publicised to death. As soon as he died, the response came in the form of pure publicity, an almost relieved acceptance that finally the damned thing had at last been resolved.

He was no good to us alive, falling apart physically and mentally, making repeated attempts to repair his image and reputation, reminding us again and again that the neurotic energy, dangerous perfectionism and desperate ambition he'd turned into dazzling, video-age show business had eventually turned back on him and started to eat him up. There was only one real way to rescue Jackson from the enduring pain of decline and reclusiveness. It wasn't going to involve taking on fifty dates at the O2 Arena, and no doubt revealing a poignant lack of wit, speed and power, and escaping to exile after a couple of disastrous shows.

When he was alive, it was never clear quite how to approach the perverse, shape-shifting, scandalous, ruined, faintly repulsive idea of Jackson, how to deal with the transformation from irresistible child star to weird, shattered, self-piteous, fallen idol. Dead, in acceptably mysterious and fairly dubious circumstances, he had joined those he had loved and admired for their life after death adventures, Garland, Dean, Monroe, Presley, Lennon, Diana – and because one of the many Michael

Jacksons seems to have had the kind of pointless, chaotic fame that we now think of as being the result of time spent on reality television, there's another chain of celebrity disaster he also belongs to that drops all the way down to *Big Brother*'s inevitably doomed Jade Goody. It was the loopy minor celebrity element there definitely is in late period, now final period, Jackson – a celebrity Big Brother appearance, even a pantomime, would have been more beneficial than all that demanding singing and dancing he was facing – that actually helped give his death something Presley's and Diana's couldn't have. An element of the busy, hustling, fragmented hyper self-aware twenty-first century, as reflected by TMZ, Fox, Perez Hilton Twitter and Google.

He'd hung on long after parts of his mind, business and body were falling off, but his sense of timing was in the end immaculate. He sprang to life in the '60s, got himself into position in the '70s between his teens and his twenties, was anointed world famous in the '80s, quickly started to disintegrate, and then hung on for dear life until the media and the web, and the way it covers itself as it covers events beyond its control, was in the right ever-vigilant, tabloid minded, freakishly amoral, multi channelled, search saturated, tweetist state to properly cover his death with the correct combination of pomp and prurience.

The media had become as bizarre in its obsessions and anxieties and worries about its image as Jackson himself. The cultural stars were in alignment. Even as he lost ultimate control he somehow took absolute control of the coverage of his life and death, disappearing behind hundreds of versions of himself, now always in our lives whether we liked the idea or not. He had been disgraced as a living legend, but death had given him back, one way or another, the kind of grace he craved. The grace that comes when your fame, and your name, cannot be taken away.

THIRTY-ONE

Quincy Jones contributed a lovely piece to the *Los Angeles Times* Calendar Section days after Michael had died. The truth was Quincy and Michael had not worked together for two decades, and even though Quincy was diplomatically quiet about what he thought had happened to him in the years since they had been together, you could guess that he was not at all impressed. He'd fallen for his focus and innocence, Michael's strategic attention to detail, when they had first met. Such things had fallen off the bus a long time ago.

Quincy understood how that time in the '80s when they all worked and dreamed together, planning their fantasies inside a studio and seeing them gush all over MTV, and the world it made, and unmade, was the perfect convergence of forces. 'We owned the '80s,' he boasted, 'and our souls would be connected forever. There will be a lot written about what came next in

Michael's life, but for me all of that is just noise. I promise you in fifty, seventy-five, a hundred years, what will be remembered is the music. It's no accident that almost three decades later, no matter where I go in the world, in every club and karaoke bar, like clockwork, you hear "Billie Jean", '"Beat It", "Wanna Be Startin' Somethin'", "Rock With You" and "Thriller".'

He knew that his construction of Michael was the ultimate reason why when Michael died it was more than just the surprise death of a celebrity. Michael Jackson could not have been considered in any form the greatest if it hadn't been for Quincy: Quincy grabbed from Michael the finer parts of his amorphous magnetism and poured it into the songs. Michael was never the same again, as though Quincy, to get that music, had needed to suck something out of Michael that severely affected his already teetering temperament. Michael needed Quincy, but Quincy needed Michael to make sense of a personal musical story that without his albums with Michael would have been missing something that made sense of everything he'd learnt. He was a Michael Jackson away from missing his moment. But Michael was a Quincy away from reaching his prime.

If Quincy, as the most sensitive and understanding of Michael's bosses, teachers, fathers, brothers, band members, aides, friends, was a primary guide, it is interesting to go back and find those that taught Quincy – to see that Michael Jackson didn't just come out of *The*

Wizard of Oz and Smokey Robinson, out of the religious fervent rural America south and the electronically groomed screaming far out. If Quincy is central to the story of Michael Jackson, or at least to a story that isn't reduced to the slimy rubble of hearsay and insinuation, a mainstream music story, then his teachers, the ones that encouraged his quest for excellence, and his own particular ruthless search for acceptance, are also important.

There was Ray Charles, his voracious carnal appetites and his juke-joint apprenticeships. Quincy would claim underground '40s trumpeter Clark Terry as an important mentor, and Count Basie as a kind of father – in the *Los Angeles* piece he mentions meeting Basie just before he died, and being so proud that Basie was so proud of him, that he'd been a jazzer that had ended up coordinating the biggest-selling album of all time.

But Quincy's more conventional teacher was a brilliant aristocratic French musician and conductor, Nadia Boulanger, known to her students as Madame, born into a musical family on 16 September 1887, who died in 1979 renowned as one of the most important composition teachers of the twentieth century. Amongst those this master musician taught: Roy Harris, John Adams, Burt Bacharach, Aaron Copland, Philip Glass, Virgil Thomson, Leonard Bernstein, Elliott Carter and Quincy, so her unlikely influence on the history of American music and its sound is considerable. She herself had been influenced by Debussy, studied composition with Gabriel Fauré, was a disciple of Ravel, and was close friends with Igor Stravinsky, who saw her as a mentor and an inspiration during his darkest days.

She considered Iannis Xenakis to be too old to teach when he approached her for lessons, and suggested he consult Olivier Messiaen. George Gershwin also approached her, but she considered there was nothing she could teach him, which he took as a compliment. Her pupils would be exhausted and depressed by the demanding rigour of her lessons, her no-nonsense assertions about talent and temperament, her craving for clarity and reason as she used music to march through time.

Conservative and highly orthodox in her approach, she apparently told Glass he would never be a composer, which actually encouraged him to prove her wrong. She told Quincy to forget about writing symphonies and concentrate on the jazz he was already making a name composing and arranging, although it's not clear whether this advice extended to pop and producing 'We Are the World'. Quincy called her strong, very strong, 'the most astounding woman I ever met in my life'.

Jones studied counterpoint, orchestration and composition under the inspirational Madame Boulanger while he was in Paris in 1957, a year before Jackson was born – meeting Picasso, James Baldwin, Josephine Baker along the way – and such studies mean that the producer of the biggest-selling pop album of all time has an intellectual approach to form and content, style and fashion, sound and meaning, energy and emotion, and can refer to Stravinsky as much as be linked to every conceivable American musical form, to Louis, Bird, Duke, Frank, Jay-Z. He understands the pure dynamics of musical decades stretching way back before the '50s and this far into the twenty-first century.

Quincy once said, 'Stravinsky said that the big responsibility of an artist is to be a great observer and really pay attention. Pay attention! The things that have guided my life are to pay attention, be true to yourself, and figure it out. That's really what it's about. My life was messed up when I was young, but so what? Get over it. Figure it out. Just inhale every second of life.'

Nadia taught him to think like this. She famously could not tolerate lack of attention. 'It is a vital part of self-awareness. It's a force of concentration and it means you do not repeat the same actions day to day. I'd go as far as saying that life is denied by lack of attention, whether it be to clean windows or write a masterpiece. I have the impression that the more I try to think about the essentials of music, the more they seem to depend on general human values. It's all very well to be a musician, it's all very well to be a genius, but the intrinsic value which constitutes your mind, your heart, your sensibility, depends on what you are. You may have to lead a life in which no one understands who you are. Nevertheless I believe that everything depends on attention. I only see you if I pay attention. I only exist in my own eyes if I pay attention to myself.'

These are some of the thoughts that Quincy would have been opened up to as taught by Madame Boulanger, a lover of Monteverdi and Bach, slipping easily from everything that came before Bach to everything that came after Stravinsky, who herself was renowned as a master of sonic precision, training her students to develop the muscles of the ear and the focus of the mind so keenly that notes, harmony, rhythms, melodies be pressed deeply into the conscious and the subconscious mind. You can imagine some of these ideas and theories being pinned up in the holy recording studio as Quincy swept up the various forces and energies that went into the making of *Off the Wall*, *Thriller* and *Bad* – some sense of something burning and moving way beyond the obvious and cynical that perhaps supplies one of the best answers to the question of why people loved this music so much, not just because of its synthetic attractiveness, electronic richness, concentrated hooks and pulsating rhythmic attack. Its jaunty, infectious force was embedded in centuries of serious musical thinking.

'To think that a man with everything against him can overcome all obstacles by courage, with will, energy, vital powers! I find that more impressive than the result itself, it's a joy to see all that effort bear fruit. And then, you must take time to savour. To eat is to taste. Stravinsky used to taste. He didn't eat fast. He savoured. I almost never taste. I eat a peach while giving a lesson and I don't notice what I eat. And then there's something extraordinary, a peach. Two years ago I had a cherry that was a masterpiece of a cherry. From time to time I think of it. I've never eaten its equal.'

'Do you know what Valery wrote? "We are told that the sea is flat, we do not see that it is standing up in front of us. It's probably the same thing with sound. It produces phenomena of the same order."'

'But the essential condition of everything you do, and not only in music, the touchstone, must be choice, love, passion. You do it because you consider the marvellous adventure of being alive depends entirely on the atmosphere you yourself create, by your enthusiasm, your conviction, your understanding.'

'Your music can never be more or less than you are as a human being.'

THIRTY-TWO

Throughout the summer, the calls kept coming, from TV, radio and newspaper, from those hoping to hire me for a few minutes, to talk about some incident generated by the after-effects of Jackson's death. Can you talk about Jackson in relation to his memorial, the fight over the children, his burial, the fact that Mark Lester is claiming he is in fact the surrogate father of two of the children, did the British kill him because he couldn't cope with the thought of performing all those London shows, what about the fact that Daddy Joe wants to create a new Jackson singing group with Michael's kids, a whole new family business, what about his doctor having all that propofol delivered to his girlfriend's apartment, what about the *Ben Hur* show and Robbie Williams taking over some of his dates at the O2 Arena, what do you think of those who want their O2 tickets as a souvenir, prepared to pay £75 for a ticket that now won't mean show number thirty-four of the Michael Jackson season, what about the Jackson benefit show, the tribute show that Jermaine is arranging, the way that the Jackson family seemed to be setting their sights cheap and cabaret low in terms of the way they carried the torch forward, Madonna calling him the greatest artist that ever lived, delivering an emotional speech at the MTV Video Music Awards, feeling he was abandoned, we all abandoned him, and put him in a box, and labelled him a strange person, what did I think of that, apparently she can't stop thinking about him, we should have helped him, how could we have helped him, does that mean he's set some weird kind of precedent, is she sincere, is she guilty about something? (A talk radio jockey responds to Madonna's proposal that we should have helped Jackson with a curt 'Speak for yourself'.)

I get the feeling that the requests will come forever, that there will always be some reverberation that requires instant pundit commentary – just how great was Jackson – the greatest? An Ali, an Otis, a Diana, a

Welles, or how about Heath Ledger; just how important is he as a man, an entertainer, what do you think of the rehearsal footage of him, as he prepared himself for the O2 shows, did he seem ready, did you hear that in fact according to the post-mortem he was all things considered relatively healthy for a man of his age suffering his levels of stress and considering the drugs he was addicted to?

I reply to some of the requests, explaining at some length that I have nothing to say or I don't know what to think about Michael Jackson and his casket, or Michael Jackson and the troubled tribute shows, or Michael Jackson and his wills. I take some time to run through all my thinking about Jackson, how I'm sloppy with chronology, I'm not the right person to summarise his contribution, I don't really like his music – this thought was often greeted at the other end of the phone as though I had in fact said Shakespeare was not as good a writer as J. K. Rowling – I can't keep a straight face, Quincy was the key, the Jacksons that are left are a disaster, La Toya makes me especially nervous. The truth is, I end up saying, I have nothing at all to say about Michael Jackson.

I get a little paranoid and feel that these producers and researchers calling me to book me on to some show to fuel or diffuse or scoff at some new piece of Jackson-associated peculiarity get a little annoyed at me playing games with them, as if they've worked out that I'm still stuck playing tedious old-fashioned games of self-reflexivity – nervous of letting go and being exposed as someone who for all his reputation as a pop writer has nothing original, surprising or relevant to say about this pop event of the year. I'm pretending I've got nothing to say even as in fact I can't shut up pushing forward various responses and theories. God, I think they think, my paranoia no doubt inflated by flying close to the palpitating Jackson paranoia, I probably still believe in that fashionable post-Nietzschean French nonsense – there are no facts, only interpretation. No one essential truth, only overlapping truths. All this deferral, but yet really not deferral, the deferring of deferring, all this spinning around, all this self-consciousness about committing myself to an actual conclusion about whether I do or do not like/admire/miss/resist/hate/understand Jackson, all this clotting up of decision and then indecision, this elaborate avoidance, this ironic evasion – it's like Camille Paglia said years ago, about all the men that get up to this game-playing nonsense, it signifies an alienation from emotion. Could there be anything worse than a fifty-odd-year-old male white rock critic fascinated by Foucault and Derrida, those blasted Eros-killers? Like she said, as an attitude towards life it betrays a perpetual adolescence.

Actually, that must make me ideally qualified to talk about Michael Jackson, even though I'm trapped inside all this anxiety about whether/if/when/how I commit to an argument, an opinion, a simple anecdotal statement, an artless, outspoken opinion. I worry that I'm giving too much away, or not giving enough away, that I don't know where to begin, and actually have no idea what it all means and where it will all end.

I reject all the requests to talk about Michael Jackson. I stop even replying to the messages. I have nothing to say about Michael Jackson. There is no actual Michael Jackson to actually say anything about, not in the ways we like to think.

Then I agree to write this essay.

THIRTY-THREE

I sometimes wondered whether Michael Jackson ever considered what kind of fuss would be made when he died, and then after. Did he spend time calculating whether he could have any kind of influence over the reaction to his death, as if it was something that could end with a virtual burst of rapturous applause, mixed with such shock that he could pull off such a move, so profoundly threaten his internal balance, produce such a climactic acknowledgement of the limits of his consciousness?

I wondered whether in his haywire and exotic later years, with the assured if battered instincts and perceptions of someone whose entire existence was based around thinking and behaving as a watched and available entertainer, he considered that it was more likely that his best chance for a glorious, life-affirming comeback, a flamboyant reconfirmation of his powers, would be to die in circumstances that were sad, seedy and suitably sensational. To die would be to live.

How carefully did he consider the idea that a certain sort of death, one achieved in a kind of privacy that was also completely public, would lead to the greatest encore of all, one that could last for ever? A peaceful relatively ordinary death, at a time of life some would consider acceptable, might not be the best way of sealing his myth. He needed to die fairly young, sadly before his time – or biblically old, decades after his time, way beyond a hundred years, encased in hi-tech sonar-fuelled technological life support and surgically transformed into a nerveless, sexless, odourless sheet of transparent skin – to complete the tragic meta-theatrical arc of a life grievously distorted by the weirdest of appetites and impulses.

This did not mean he would take his own life, not directly, not with desperate, shattered purpose, a final smack of ferocious focus, not as an explicit premeditated act of escape intended to release him from merciless pain and misery. Nothing that cynical, if suicide can be called cynical. It would mean that he was aware that the death of someone like Michael Jackson – his own death, allowing for the fact that he maintained a connection to himself, to the fact that he was Michael Jackson, even as he had peeled away from the idea that he actually was Jackson, living inside that skin, inside that reputation – would be a crucial conclusion to his life-as-performance, and that the way he exits the stage, leaving an audience with a last tantalising sight of his presence, would have an enormous impact on how he is remembered.

For someone as famous as Jackson, for someone who has managed to make the whole world a stage, someone so terribly self-conscious about making people aware of him, to the point that he seemed content to allow people to become aware of him because he was weird and distressed, death is a major part of the whole strategy. Death is everything, because it will ensure that everything he fought for, to be so alive millions of people would know all about how alive he was, would not lead to nothing. Death would be a key element in ensuring no one ever forgot how hard he worked as an entertainer to let people know he was alive.

Did he think a lot about what form his death would take, and what unpleasant kind of death would be the most useful in how it contributed to maintaining enough interest in him, as extreme pop star, celebrity fiend and object of fascination, so that he would not, if you think about it, die? He would simply make one more altera-tion in his appearance, one more conceptual adjustment in how he presented himself to the world. His death would be the extravagant equivalent of an outrageously manipulative costume change, a stunning example of spine-tingling performance magic that would ensure no one would ever forget the name Michael Jackson.

Did he spend much time dwelling on how and when, and why, he died would have a huge impact on his post-humous reputation, and so therefore the design of his death, whether accidental or intentional, was as import-ant a part of what it was he did as any piece of music, as any video, television interview or award ceremony? Was there some kind of personal preference for how he died, a sense that the more mysterious and suspicious his death, the better it would be for the life he would lead once he was dead – a strange, murky Los Angeles death announced first by a celebrity website and then distributed around the news world in sensational pomp-filled seconds, a fitting death for someone whose life ulti-mately seemed like one long preparation for a squalid, endlessly analysed and ultimately expressive departure?

Did he anticipate how he would be remembered, and hope that the coverage of his death would mean that he was honoured for his glossy, tremendous music and erupt-ive movement, and not the kinkiness and decadence, his attempts to be normal and live a normal life which ended up merely intensifying his abnormality, his inability to function? Did he ever dream of just what would happen to his body, who and what would be the first outlet or organisation to make the announcement, would he be on his own when he died, surrounded by family, or in the middle of a sudden panicky flight to exile?

Perhaps the moment would come when he was on his own in a penthouse suite in Las Vegas after a 2034 comeback that seemed chilling and yet heroic in its recreation of late twentieth-century show business perfection. A common, anti-climactic heart attack. Perhaps a successful assassination by someone or some organisation he had defiled or let down – a late payment on some mammoth loan he entered into, so he could maintain his decaying Neverland home.

The worst thing of all, from the point of view of his reputation, would be to die of natural causes. By being Michael Jackson he naturally required supernatural causes.

Perhaps he knew, even to the extent of indirectly setting up the circumstances, that his death would have to be appallingly grim, an unstoppable descent into darkness, and unbearable lightness, due to a chaotic combination of sedatives, anaesthetics and painkillers, a few days before his big, improbable comeback was due to take off, leaving open the necessary myth generating possibilities that it could have been murder, suicide, fake, accident, full of alleged this and alleged that, and even just the result of a certain lack of concentration, an amount of neglect from those paid to look after him on an ordinary afternoon that suddenly became extraordinary.

THIRTY-FOUR

I saw Michael Jackson die. That's not quite the exact truth, but then as Michael Jackson sort of sang, nothing ever really is. While he was alive, there was nothing exactly true about Michael Jackson, nothing that could ever make you think, that's who Michael Jackson is, he is that one thing, and only that. He is simply what his name, and his successful compelling popular music, makes you think he is. He is no more and no less than what he wants us to think he is.

And then, because he died, and I saw it happen, in my own home, spread over time, a turbulent mind-boggling decline reaching a sudden unavoidable climax, you could now not work out the truth of what he had been, who he was, exactly how he would be remembered. There was no exact truth, perhaps, because there were too many near truths, all of them competing with each other, all of them with the same weight, the same value, the same level of integrity, the same lack of integrity, the same gigantic transparency.

Or there was no exact truth because there was nothing true, and truly settled, about Michael Jackson and his relationship to the rest of us, a relationship which ended with his death, which I witnessed. Michael Jackson lived, and died, sang, and danced, at the edge of reason, and so far out was his life and death that everything about him was a construct built out of lies, rumours, publicity, hints, avoidance, revelation and perversity. Everything about him was a lie, an evasion, an escape, a revenge, an outrage, and here perhaps was an ultimate example of how distinctive entertainers essentially find a way to tell risky even dangerous lies about themselves and their lives in order to seduce those less prepared to so comprehensively make up their identity. The great entertainers invent themselves so thoroughly that there is little about them that is in any ordinary sense solid and stable.

The great entertainer vibrates with predatory slyness and subterfuge, even as they find ways to present this surreptitious energy as a sincere kind of generosity and humility. They appear to give everything they are in order to entertain and amuse the masses. Really, they are always taking, feeding their neediness with the love and attention of their audience. Their whole act is continually a lie, and is always about finding ways to camouflage this lie, this dazzling forgery, as something reliable. Entertainment is a way of disguising necessary deception and a consistent fabrication as something honourable and honest, and Jackson symbolised how trying to keep that arrangement going at the level he was at can often lead to the entertainment, and the entertainer, buckling under the pressure.

I think as soon as I saw Jackson die, on my television, in my imagination, or at least as soon as it was announced that he had died, a death that had been building up since he was a boy, or even a baby, or even before, I started to wonder just what the truth was. About the death, which was obviously an interesting kind of death because I had seen it happen, and it was an infected grandiose drama, and it was built in the image of famous assassinations, dubious accidents, cryptic deaths, possible suicides, bizarre comas, blatantly the kind of death with implied causes, suggestive anomalies and a whiff of the criminal that would never be solved, and I don't think I was alone in seeing it unfold, but also about the life. I couldn't help it.

I started to have thoughts about whether it would ever be possible to understand the truth about someone who was so embedded in the idea of show business as a sort of seductive fraudulence. Now that he was dead, would some sort of truth take shape, because, after all, the death seemed true enough? Or would the death take us further and further away from truth, because, after all, his death may now be a fact, but it was soon apparent that this was the kind of death that is not about truth, but about the kind of distortion, disinformation, small talk and mercenary exaggeration that is at the heart of all commercial entertainment? This death was still part of the process of building an image, of continuing the work of shepherding his manufactured presence and the soundtrack and accompanying images that are at the heart of the fabrication into whatever shops will be like in the future. He was born to be bought, and in death it will still be all about customers, and consumers, and souvenir hunters.

Within seconds of his death, which was televised, live,

more or less, people around the world started to talk about Michael Jackson, about his nebulous, disordered life, and then about the death which had the appearance of something oddly methodical, as if it had been previously measured so that it would achieve maximum promotional impact. There was certainly something to talk about, and those that were talking, the newsreaders and then the pundits, guests and those that claimed to be friends quickly called upon to offer thoughts and reflections, seemed ready to summarise the reputation, music and demented family life of Michael Jackson, as if it was relatively straightforward. They talked as if there was a way of seeing truth, or at least working towards the truth, about this character, and the way his whole life meant that in the end he would die, live, on TV, hidden from view, but as exposed as anything. And, clearly, there was now someone to cherish, to praise, to honour, a good, decent man, someone who cared about the less fortunate and deserving, who was selfless and giving, not the soft-voiced, evasive, self-indulgent mega has-been dedicated to building an entertainment empire as if there was something of the Walt Disney about him.

THIRTY-FIVE

Michael Jackson is buried with full make-up on, wearing his precious white glove and sunglasses, draped in beads and pearls with a huge gold belt around his waist.

THIRTY-SIX

As soon as Michael Jackson died, he came to life. As soon as he stopped, he started. The whole thing, this awful conclusion to a life spent spiralling into chaos – this freaky circus event, this historic item of news, this pure emblazoning blast of transmitted energy based on a momentarily unbelievable piece of information – was timed to perfection, suggesting that the essence of life, of existence, of maintaining balance, of locating and projecting charisma, is all about timing. At his very best, Jackson was a master of timing, of moving his body through space in a series of considered spontaneous sequences that indicated he was in so much control of his existence he could do whatever he wanted. Look how he moved, a vision of self-control, a genius at turning emotion into movement. At his devastating, distressing worst, he was confounded by time, and couldn't keep up with it. It broke him up. He could barely move. It surrounded him and took away his freedom. At the moment he died, time had taken all the power away from him, but he hadn't given up entirely. As soon as he died, there he was, facing up to time, and moving in a whole new way. He'd planned it that way, that the moment of death was not the end. It was where the story of Michael Jackson really began. Everything before the death was part of the getting ready.

He died. It was a kind of performance, as much a part of his career as a brash, exuberant early '70s Motown single, a flash, sophisticated massive selling Quincy Jones album, a frail but feisty post-'90s comeback, a startling near-sickening surgical adjustment, a self-consciously semi-crazed TV interview. We couldn't see his death, it was the most hidden thing of all, beyond even the reach of the scandal-hunters and celebrity-chasers, but we could imagine the moment, fantasise about how he made the move from one original state to altogether another, marvel at the final sounds he heard, and his final thoughts.

Perhaps his final thoughts were something Quincy had once told him Madame Nadia Boulanger had said: 'Nothing is better than music. When it takes us out of time, it has done more for us than we have the right to hope for. It has broadened the limits of our sorrowful lives: it has lit up the sweetness of our hours of happiness by effacing the pettinesses that diminish us. It brings us back to the pure and new.'

Or maybe something of his own: 'If you enter this world knowing you are loved and you leave this world knowing the same, then everything that happens in between can be dealt with.'

Or something Paris Hilton once said: 'Of course it will work. I am a marketing genius.'

THIRTY-SEVEN

There are thoughts I had about Michael Jackson before he died, and there are thoughts I am having now that he is dead. Some of these thoughts are the same, and some are very different – there are those thoughts you could only have when he was alive, when there are still all sorts of absurd, amazing possibilities about how such a life can proceed, and those thoughts you can only have when he has died, and one set of possibilities are replaced by another. There are the thoughts you can have about how the body of Michael Jackson changed while he was alive, and how the body changed once he was dead. There are the thoughts you can have about an enslaved Michael Jackson slogging through 2009 and into 2010 performing night after night, month after month, at the O2 arena, a constant cycle of pretence, strain and frazzled razzle-dazzle that the poor bamboozled media couldn't keep up with, as if Jackson was using the shows to overwhelm them with his presence until they were unbelievably forced to actually ignore him. Or he was using the show to pay off debts, to pay off the crooks, banks, courts and blackmailers, so that each show was his way of printing enough cash to fulfil his financial obligations and stay alive and perhaps have enough left over at the end to withdraw to Neverland and never, ever, ever, ever leave. One final amount of enforced work, the kind of grinding fleet-footed blank-eyed routine and sweat that was the desperate middle-aged version of the chained child star efforts, and then some freedom, the rest of his life, where he could design the perfect sort of exotic superstar exile and let the myths and rumours about the length of his fingernails, the state of his skin, the job requirements of his nurses, masseurs and maids, the number of caged wild animals, the songs he'd been working on for thirty-four years and the peculiar architecture of the underground cells he slept in grow until they completely buried him.

There are the thoughts you can have about how the overbooked, overstretching *This Is It* shows he was apparently preparing for, in all good, fit and healthy faith, were a complete distraction from his real plans. *This Is It* was Jackson's last and greatest act of misdirection – everyone was looking that way, where he seemed to be setting up the show, the flashiest trick of all, the biggest of his showbiz dares, where he was hiring the dancers, musicians, sorting out the set list, developing the arrangements of the songs, rehearsing his moves, selling the tickets, attending the launch, confounding those that thought he was not up to it, seemingly laughing in the face of all the doubt and suspicion and the accusations, working on the comeback show of all comeback shows that would prove once and for all that he was the mighty eternal king, ruler and creator of all pop culture he surveyed, and not now simply the pitiful, repulsive curio heading for the shopping channels, and outmanoeuvred by the likes of Miley Cyrus, the Jonas Brothers and the Pussycat Dolls.

While we are all looking that way, beginning against our better judgement to believe that he might actually be serious about undertaking this impossible, unprecedented marathon, he was somewhere else altogether in a very different frame of mind. He was planning a very different sort of *This Is It*, a very different way of spending the rest of 2009, and indeed the rest of his life. Perhaps for a while he really did engage with the idea of announcing just how physically and mentally limber he was by lightly knocking off these fifty shows, completing something that even in these jaded times would be considered to be awesome. Perhaps he really did conceive of the technological methods where stand-ins, models and holographic versions of various Jacksons could be used, so that his fans weren't disappointed. He could invent the kind of show involving electronically faithful reproductions and genetically modified Jacksons that once more confirmed how ahead of his showbiz time he was, anticipating how to produce a convincing meta-Vegas show that could run forever as an official Michael Jackson Production even if he was not actually physically a part of it. All about him, featuring nothing of his that was real.

Deep down, he was fully aware that there was no chance he could put himself through so much pain and pressure, no matter how physically strong he might actually be, regardless of how ingenious the multidimensional representation of his music and dancing was. He could not coast through these shows, miming, sending along body doubles, hiding behind a tidal surge of special effects. He was risking losing everything, and becoming a laughing stock, reducing his show business currency to the value of Milli Vanilli and Vanilla Ice.

He willingly let the financial and practical reality of the shows, the expectation and anticipation, gather so much momentum that the whole plan engulfed him. He allowed himself to be cornered by the commitment that was expected from him. In the end, he let *This Is It* become something that was both a cryptic suicide note, and the abstract cause of death.

Once Michael Jackson had died, it wasn't as though he actually disappeared. He might have added a certain depth to his invisibility, but there would be no stopping the traces of visibility he'd always sent out into the world from wherever he was hiding. If there is one thing that it very clean about Michael Jackson it is that his death does not mean he has gone missing. Death has not plunged him into anonymity. Death has put an absolute stop to the idea that Michael Jackson can ever be inconspicuous.

It wasn't as though his death meant we stopped thinking about him. It just meant that we thought about him in a different way, and in fact one of the first thoughts I had when I found out that he had died, as my thoughts about a living Jackson started to mingle with the new thoughts about a dead Jackson, was that it made more sense to be thinking about him as a dead star than as a living legend rotting by the day. As a dead star, he was pristine, he was complete, he was in his element. It was everything he was meant to be. Death had made him more real than ever. He was now the most real he had ever been.

I thought about how there were so many different versions of Michael, held by so many different people, that perhaps this was the secret of the immortality he craved for himself, and then arranged by dying at what, so the story goes, was just the right Jackohyperbolic moment. At the point of death, there were so many Jacksons that even as some were removed, as reputations and myths were debunked, as various versions started to fade away, as memories of his greatness faded, or memories of his horrible demise were erased, as some people just started forgetting, because they had other things, and other celebrities, on their minds, there were always memories and versions and highlights and a lingering love of Jackson that still existed. He could not be completely wiped away because as an idea he was multiple, and too scattered and luminous as a presence to truly disappear.

THIRTY-EIGHT

An obscure moment of silence, a final sigh, a last twitch, a catastrophic drop in temperature, an ugly scrapping of motion, and a gnarled, breathtaking pause that no one could ever know anything about. Michael Jackson, the winning singer, the celebrated mover, the worshipped hero, the accused wheeler-dealer, the soiled living legend, the warped icon, the faded legend, the troubled, scarred recluse, the savaged superstar, now all by himself, backstage, off to the side of space and time, as if everything was finished, the show was over, the curtain down, the applause given and gone, the colleagues, nurses, minders, butlers, medics and assistants let go, the lights out, the stark night stretching on forever. Now that it was all over, this grand dramatic commitment to performance, this intense self-sacrifice, after giving so much of himself, taking all the energy he could muster in the act of pleasing himself by pleasing others, it seemed like the end of the world. It seemed like he had nothing more to give. There was nothing left.

He removed his ravishing, preposterous costume. Anyone nearby would have flinched in shock. He picked out the fake hair and pulled off bits of his body artificially added to ensure he resembled a human shape even as he'd left behind the conventional proportions and colouring of a man his age, race and size. Shed with a sinister shudder the sick glitter of mortality. Lay naked, despondent and exposed inside his own incandescent isolation.

He found the kind of relieved calm he searched for all his life, and sank into himself so profoundly, the steadiness and peace he achieved rinsed away decades of pain, suffering, anxiety and chaos. He was on his own, so lonely he would never be able to explain to anyone just what it felt like to be so lonely, and so at the end of his tether. He looked in a mirror. There was no one there. The image had completely faded. He'd disappeared.

And then a sudden red-hot transformation, an electric emergence of an authorised immortality, a powerful confirmation that Jackson without the skin and bones the head and heart the tortured body and soul that had ruined him was to be somehow more than he had ever been. The curtains opening. The lights flashing on. A radiant show business commotion of pumping liquid ecstatic sound and a constant clatter of gossip.

He had arrived. He was where he belonged. Right in front of us, demanding our attention. He had stormed into our minds, where he felt instantly at home, where he could move around and manipulate our emotions and memories with ultimate freedom and flexibility.

At this moment, as a desperately needed deep sleep dissolved into an abyss, a moment so real it was something you could only describe by making up the details, something he had been preparing himself for his whole life, as if he could actually permanently postpone its occurrence, the Michael Jackson we now think of, the one that's dead and gone, was born.

This is what we had been waiting for, what he had been waiting for – one kind of death, a severe removal of necessary signs, the kind of action leading to ultimate inaction that will never be understood, a great mystery leading to perpetual rumours and endless questions, and then, immediately, this new state of being, this life after death, this new form of immaculate stardom. Some kind of survival replacing the moment he knew, deep in himself, deep in a coma of someone's making, that everything he was, this man who so easily changed his shape and skin, had made the most dramatic change of all. Michael Jackson had entered, through the darkness of some messy, miserable final moments, a different life, one that seemed instantly to hint at making sense of his role in our lives, of his tenacious, reverberating position in our imagination.

He had, after all that, found his way home. A haunted house. He shut the door. He turned out the lights. His eyes adjusted to the dark. He thought of nothing and no one. His brain stopped burning. The bass started grooving. He was in control. He didn't move a muscle.

I looked at him for a while and then I left him where he was.